OTHER BOOKS BY DAVID CLARKE

Men Are Clams, Women Are Crowbars
A Marriage After God's Own Heart
I Don't Love You Anymore

We can say that without Dr. Clarke's solid biblical counsel we might not have had a happy ending to the parenting war. If you are a parent who is wounded by friendly fire. . .coming from children who are supposed to be on your side, this book is for you! RICK CHAPELL, parent

In David Clarke's *Parenting Isn't for Superheroes,* parents will find practical guidelines and insights which will change parenting from an ordeal to be endured to an enriching experience. It's full of humor, biblical applications, and just plain common sense. HAROLD J. SALA,
President of Guidelines International,
author, and speaker

Parenting Isn't for Superheroes is a fun, fun book—you'll laugh hilariously at your own life. David Clarke is insightful, practical, and very vulnerable, as well as funny.
JIM CONWAY, PH.D.,
President, Midlife Dimensions,
and author of *Men in Midlife Crisis,*
Women in Midlife Crisis,
and *Traits of a Lasting Marriage*

If you really love your kids, take the time to read this book. *Parenting Isn't for Superheroes* is a great combination of humor and Bible-based wisdom. Dr. Clarke's personal approach and creative strategies will help you raise healthy kids who love you and love the Lord. DAVID AND CLAUDIA ARP,
Co-founders of Marriage Alive and authors of
Suddenly They're 13 and *Love Life for Parents*

PARENTING ISN'T FOR SUPER HEROES

Everyday Strategies for Raising Good Kids

DAVID CLARKE, Ph.D.

BARBOUR BOOKS
An Imprint of Barbour Publishing, Inc.

© 2003 by David Clarke, Ph.D.

ISBN 1-58660-727-8

Cover image © Artville

Published by Barbour Books, an imprint of Barbour Publishing, Inc., P.O. Box 719, Uhrichsville, Ohio 44683, www.barbourbooks.com

 Member of the
Evangelical Christian
Publishers Association

Printed in the United States of America.
5 4 3 2 1

Acknowledgments

- Sandy Clarke, my wife, my love, my life, and one terrific mom.

- Emily, Leeann, Nancy, and William Clarke, I love being your dad. Thanks for being such great kids.

- Bill and Kathy Clarke, the greatest parents in the world. Thanks for everything. Thanks, also, Dad, for all your work on the manuscript.

- Kermit and Jean Martin, thanks for raising the most wonderful person in the world, my wife.

- Ethel Harris, my right-hand woman. You make a big difference in my life.

- Ed Harris, a godly man, husband, and father. Your love for your family is an example for us all.

- Gary Gaertner, thanks for your work in typing the first part of the manuscript.

- Denise Hall, my trusted research assistant and great friend. You came through in the pinch.

- Rocky Glisson, my great friend and fellow prayer warrior.

- Susan Schlabach, thanks for asking. I appreciate all you've done for me.

- God, my precious, loving, heavenly Father. All I have, You have given to me.

Contents

Introduction

When you make the choice to have children, my friends, you give up many things.

You give up your money. Kids are incredibly expensive. You've got to feed them, clothe them, transport them, doctor them, educate them, and entertain them.

Children are, in every sense of the word, consumers. Your home is filled—right now—with expensive toys, clothes, and shoes that your kids don't even use! Am I right? Yes, I am. You'll find me right about so many things.

I don't know about you, but I'm sick and tired of buying shoes for my four kids that fit only for a week or two. It's not right! It's ridiculous! It's costing me serious money!

Some time ago, my thirteen-year-old daughter, Emily, needed some new shoes. Fine. No problem. I held a brief meeting in the kitchen with Emily and my lovely wife, Sandy. I told Sandy to buy shoes for Emily that were big and loose. Shoes that literally slipped and flapped when she walked. That way, she could grow into them. Sandy said, "Yes, sir." Okay, she didn't say that. But she agreed to buy shoes that were plenty big. Off they went to the mall.

When they returned, we had another meeting in the kitchen. Not that I didn't trust Sandy, but I had to make sure Emily's new shoes were big enough. I did the old thumb test and, hallelujah, there was plenty of room in her shoes. We were all very happy. Not even two weeks later, Emily came up to me in the hallway wearing her new shoes and said, "Dad, I need some new shoes. These shoes are too tight."

I couldn't believe it! "What do you mean, too tight? We bought those thirty-dollar shoes less than two weeks ago!" I said, in a high-pitched voice. "Look, kid. I don't care if they cripple your feet. You're wearing those shoes for at least a month!"

I didn't say that. Oh, I wanted to, believe me. I said what every parent says in that situation, "Where's my checkbook?" We went back to the mall to buy Emily another pair of brand-new shoes. My kids have more shoes than Imelda Marcos. And none of them fit! (You remember Imelda, the wife of the former president of the Philippines. She had thousands and thousands of shoes in her palace. At least Imelda's shoes fit.)

When one of my four kids asks for something we can't afford, I say, "Years ago, your dear mother and I had a choice: have money or have children. Look around, kiddo, and you'll see the choice we made."

When you make the choice to have children, you also give up your food. As they grow, children eat more and more, which of course leaves you with less and less. You see, until children are twenty-one years of age, the part of their brains that tells them they're full is not fully developed. And so, they will eat until there is no food left. Like cows grazing in a pasture, your children will strip your home of food. At least, the food that tastes good. They will leave behind vegetables, prunes, and whole wheat bread sticks. Funny how that works.

The part of their brains that tells them to avoid your special snack food—candy, ice cream, that last piece of cake—is also not fully developed. You've been dreaming all day of that one special candy bar you've hidden in the freezer. You've had a hard day. You want that bar. You need that bar. It's your bar! The success or failure of your entire day rests upon that one little bar. You go through your day, come home, play with the kids, and eat dinner. Then, you walk to the freezer door with confidence and anticipation. You smile as you imagine biting into your bar and tasting that smooth, creamy chocolate.

You open the door and your bar is. . .gone! It's not there! You frantically rummage around, but you must face the brutal truth: There will be no bar for you tonight. You shut the freezer door, turn, and see on the floor the empty wrapper of your bar. Well, you know what's happened. You don't even bother asking your kids. They'd just lie. Just like they've lied before. With the chocolate from your bar smeared on their faces, they'd say, "Chocolate bar? No, we didn't see a chocolate bar, Daddy." Liars! Cheats! Sneak thieves!

Finally, here is the cruelest blow of all. When you have children, you give up your sex. Remember sex? Remember how much fun it was before the children came along? I do. Oh, yes, I do. It's a cruel paradox. You must have sex to have children. But then, once you have children, you have no more sex! It's over.

The two of you are reduced to scheduling sex in ten- to fifteen-minute periods at odd hours: when the kids are asleep or out of your hair. Which is practically never! "Look, honey, how about next Wednesday morning, from 1:00 A.M. to 1:15 A.M.? What do you think?" It's pathetic, that's what it is. The only good thing about this lack of sex is that it prevents you from having more children—which would lead to even less sex!

No one warns us that we're giving all this up. Our parents just whine for grandchildren, as though it's their right. They say nothing, because they know if we knew the truth, we'd never have kids. After we have kids, then they smirk, laugh out loud, and say, "Now you know what it's like!" These are bitter, petty people! They don't want grandchildren for pleasure. They want them for revenge!

Even though all this is true, if you're like Sandy and me, you wouldn't trade your kids for anything. And—really—their grandparents love them, too. Seriously, children give back far more than they take.

- They are blessings from God.
- They're fun.
- They enrich us.
- They give life new meaning.
- They are the future.

Because our children are so precious to us, we want them to grow up happy and healthy. But just wanting healthy kids won't make it happen. You've got to do things right as a parent. Specifically, you've got to do six things right.

- The first thing is to realize parenting isn't for superheroes.

Superheroes battle archenemies. You're in a war with your own kids! Kids are selfish, fiendishly inventive, and naturally gravitate to behaviors that are bad for them. They'll fight you at every turn, test your patience to its limit, and may break your heart with poor decisions.

But you're also in a war with society for the hearts and minds of your children. There was a time when society actually provided support for parents. We had certain standards and moral codes that were part of our cultural fabric. That time is gone. Our culture is not deteriorating. It has already deteriorated. Just look around. Our culture's message is loud and clear: Anything goes, because there are no rules.

When you're in a war, you need a battle plan. You won't win the war without one. The other five things you must do right as a parent are the five elements of my battle plan:

- Identify and adjust your parenting style.
- Work on four key relationships.
- Meet your child's five critical needs.
- Create a no-nonsense, behavior-based system of discipline.
- Respond effectively to the five earthshaking changes every teenager goes through.

If you can learn to do these five things successfully, you can win the parenting war. You can build a great kid. A kid with healthy, God-centered self-esteem. A kid who is responsible, independent, and able to develop good relationships. A kid who will be a great friend of yours as an adult. A kid who will impact society—and not the other way around. Most importantly, a kid who will love Jesus Christ and serve Him.

ONE

Gifts from God— or Instruments of Slow Torture?

Parenting Is Hard, and Then You Die

There is one question that has haunted parents for centuries. Here it is: Are children gifts from God—or instruments of slow torture? Actually, they are both. Parenting has moments of wonder, excitement, and enrichment—broken up by long stretches of exasperation, total chaos, and suffering.

As you begin parenthood with a newborn baby, you just want this little person to survive. You sneak into the nursery every thirty minutes to make sure the little thing is still breathing. You meet every need of this small, helpless creature.

When your child hits the twos and threes and is systematically destroying your home—piece by broken piece—you begin to wonder if *you* will survive.

When your child moves into junior high and becomes a teenager, you know you're not going to make it. You realize with horror that the roles are reversed: You are now a small, helpless creature at the mercy of a far superior force: hormones.

If you and your ungrateful, hostile, and attitude-challenged teenager survive through high school, two things happen. One, your health is broken. Two, you must now spend your retirement savings on college. Talk about a gamble! All that money for a kid you're not even sure is going to turn out well.

With your health broken and your money spent, you

must spend your declining years praying that one of your kids will have pity on you and take care of you. That's the main reason Sandy and I had four kids. We figure at least one of them will look after us when we're in our wheelchair years.

This brief overview of the parenting process is tongue-in-cheek. But there is truth to it, isn't there? Parenting is an extremely difficult job. Just about impossible, really. It seems as though we are often at the mercy of our children. Once they get out of diapers, kids can cut quite a swath of destruction and mayhem through our lives.

Parents Who Feel Powerless

Many parents I've talked to tell me they feel powerless and insignificant. They believe they have virtually no influence on the lives of their children. This feeling of helplessness has caused them to abandon their God-given role of leading, motivating, shaping, and guiding their children. They are no longer parents. They are spectators.

Here are statements I've heard from many parents:

- "Nothing we do makes an impact."
- "I just can't get through to my child."
- "I'm exhausted, frustrated, burned-out, and I quit."
- "There's not much we can do except hang on for the ride."
- "We're just hoping and praying our kids turn out well."

Ever felt this way? Ever said things like this? Join the club. And it's a big club. Every parent, if he or she is honest, has reached this point more than once. There are times Sandy and I have just wanted to pack up and move to a cabin on top of a mountain in the middle of nowhere. Just the two of us. Without leaving our children a forwarding address.

Parents Who Make the Difference

But we haven't quit. We haven't given up. And neither should you. Because even though it's easy to believe we are weak and powerless as parents, it is not true. My fellow parents, listen to me. We can do a lot as parents. The truth is, we do make the difference in the lives of our children. We have the power and the authority from God Himself to determine how our children turn out as adults. Don't just take my word for it. Listen to what God says in Proverbs 22:6:

> *"Train a child in the way he should go,*
> *and when he is old he will not turn from it."*

There are two central truths in this verse I want to highlight. First, God is saying that parents can raise healthy kids. We can do it! We can train our children to grow up and live as wise, godly adults.

Second, and very importantly, God is saying that to produce a great kid you must follow a plan. You must have a clear and proper course of action. You don't hope for the best. You purposefully carry out your parenting plan. And, most of the time, your children will turn out beautifully.

A Parenting Strategy That Works!

What you need, my friends, is a parenting strategy. A practical, carefully researched, and Bible-based strategy. A strategy that has been proven to work. It just so happens, I have such a strategy.

What you'll read in this book is the way my parents raised my brother Mark—who is a pastor—and me, and so far, we've turned out pretty well. It is the way Sandy and I are raising our four children. It's the way I've taught thousands of parents, in my therapy office and in my seminars, to raise their kids. It isn't a perfect strategy. It does not contain all the truth in the universe about parenting. It just works.

Your Style Is Cramping Your Kid

My strategy begins with your parenting style. The first thing you must do to be a successful parent is identify and adjust your parenting style. You're thinking, *I didn't know I had a parenting style.* Well, you do. Your parenting style is your behavior and attitude as a parent. It's based on your personality and how you were raised.

No one is by nature a perfect parent. In fact, by nature, we each have a built-in parenting style that is not healthy for our children. I'm just full of good news, am I not?

We can't change the fact that we have this style. What we can do is find out what our parenting style is and make adjustments. That's a huge part of good parenting. I'm going to help you do that. And you're going to thank me for it, believe me.

Let's take a close look at five common parenting styles. I'll describe the characteristics of each style, the message that style sends to the child, and the impact on the child. And I'll describe the solution—how you can begin to adjust.

When you're finished reading the styles, if you can't figure out which one you have, just ask your spouse. He or she will know. Or ask a close friend or family member. Better yet, ask your children. They'd love to tell you what kind of parent you are. Also, you may find that you have more than one of these dysfunctional parenting styles. That's okay. Don't panic. It's perfectly normal. You're not strange or terribly deviant. (You might be strange, but it isn't because of this.) As a matter of fact, most parents have at least two of these styles.

Safe, but Suffocated:
The Overprotective Parent

"Let Me Do It, Honey"

You do everything for your child. You wake him up in the morning. You pick out his clothes. You comb his hair. You put the toothpaste on his toothbrush. You make breakfast for him. Look, the kid can get his own bowl, cereal, toast, and milk. What are you running, a diner?

You keep his room clean. You do his homework, don't you? You do the math. You write the reports. All your kid has to do is whine, "I can't do it," or, "I don't understand." And like the Great Mother Teresa of Education, you swoop in and take care of it.

You're back in school, and you're doing quite well. You ought to be. It's fourth-grade material—or whatever grade your kid is in at school. Who's in school here? You, or your kid? I spoke to a lady once who admitted, rather sheepishly, that she wrote all her elementary school son's reports. She actually imitated his handwriting and made mistakes on purpose so the teacher would think it was her son's work. Is that pathetic or what?

If grades mean more to you than they do to your kid, something's wrong. The something wrong is you, being over-protective. I know many parents, mostly moms, who do way too much homework for their child all the way through high school. On graduation day, these moms should get the diplomas! They earned them.

It's okay to help your child with schoolwork, but don't do it for him. You're not in school. He is. If you do too much, he won't learn spit; he'll end up a dunce. When he gets to college, what's going to happen? Unless you're going to live with him in the dorm, he's going to be in big trouble.

"Please Be Careful"

You continually warn your child of the dangers in the world and limit activities and interests outside the home. You prefer to keep your child safe at home with you. You don't like youth sports. Football, baseball, soccer, and hockey are dangerous games, and there's too high of a risk of injury. You can reel off a list of fifteen kids who have gotten injured in a sport. "Mike down the street got hit in the eye with a baseball." "Susan Searcy broke her leg in that soccer league last summer." "Timmy Cracklemeyer wasn't wearing his athletic supporter in the last football game and some monster gave him a nasty kick. The poor kid walked like a duck for a month."

You're just sure that your kid will suffer some horrible injury if you allow her to participate in a sport. You say, "No, you might get hurt." Well, of course, she might get hurt. Lots of things might happen anywhere. But each year, there are far more accidents in the home than on playgrounds and athletic fields.

You also won't let your child go on sleepovers. You can't take the chance. "I know you're seventeen, but we just don't know the Smiths well enough." Come on, now, it's time to loosen up. Check out the friend. Check out the parents.

Make sure they're not some biker couple. Determine if their home could be a bad influence. Then, let your kid go and spend the night. Sleepovers can begin in second grade and continue through high school. Not only do sleepovers foster independence, but they get the kid out of the house and leave you and your spouse alone! Or at least with one kid fewer.

You overprotective parents are fearful. You worry twenty-four hours a day. Every time your kid leaves home, you call out, "Please be careful!" If your kid is ten minutes late getting home, you're calling the hospitals. You give too much help. You hold your child too close. You are suffocating your child!

This is easy to do in our world. It is scary and dangerous out there. Bad things do happen. But we cannot completely protect our kids from all the bad, painful possibilities. If we go too far in our efforts to shield them from the world, we do our kids much more harm than good. We're trying to protect them, but we end up hurting them.

As a dad of three girls, I have been guilty of being over-protective. I want my sweeties to be safe; I don't want them hurt by anyone or anything. When my Emily was four years old, our church choir director asked us if she could sing a solo as part of a children's choir performance. My reaction was immediate: "What? A solo? In front of the whole church? By herself? Are you crazy? She isn't ready for that! She might get humiliated!"

As usual, my wife Sandy was the voice of reason. She told me Emily had the ability and the poise to do the solo. Sandy was convinced this would be good for Emily's confidence. And, she added, Emily could use her gift from God, her voice, by performing. Well, I didn't like it. But I couldn't very well argue against Emily using her gift in God's service.

I was a wreck the day of the performance. I fretted, worried, and chewed my nails all the way through Emily's solo. She carried it off beautifully and we were very proud. If I'd gotten my way, I would have robbed Emily of an opportunity to boost her self-esteem and serve God.

"You Can't Make It on Your Own"

This is the message you overprotective parents are sending to your child: "You can't make it on your own." You don't mean to send it. You don't even realize you're sending it. But you are, every day, in many ways.

What's the impact of this message on your child? Your child tends to lose initiative and motivation, because he's not allowed to do much! He has no faith in his own abilities because he isn't allowed to practice and improve them. Your child will have great difficulty breaking away and becoming independent. Why? Because you've not taught independence.

Let me ask you a question. When your children grow to adulthood, do you want them to live at home with you? I hope not! You want to get rid of them! I mean, release them. That sounds better. But, instead, you are creating dependent persons.

Welcome to the Real World

Your home is not real life. Real life is out there. You cannot shelter your children forever. Sooner or later, they'll be out there in the real world. The only question is, will you have prepared them adequately for our world? Our sinful, selfish, Satan-controlled world.

You have to expose your kids to the world. If you don't,

you set them up for failure. They won't have a chance. Satan loves to get his hands on overprotected kids. He beats them up and damages them before they can adjust to the harsh realities of our culture. So take steps to toughen up your kids. Life is hard and they need to get used to it.

Sandy and I faced a very difficult decision in 1998. We had to decide whether to leave our two oldest daughters, Emily and Leeann, in their private Christian school or put them in public school. It was an agonizing time for us—and for Emily and Leeann. They had been at a Christian school for years and they were very happy there. It was a safe, secure, and nurturing environment. The teachers were great. There were many godly role models for the kids to observe. Emily and Leeann received excellent Bible teaching. Jesus Christ was at the center of the curriculum.

There were just two problems. One, we could no longer afford the tuition. As you might imagine, money was the initial reason for our educational dilemma. But as we talked and prayed, both as a couple and as a family, Sandy and I realized there was a second problem with this wonderful Christian school. It was not real life.

The kids' school was a lot like our home: populated by very nice people who loved Jesus Christ and treated the girls with love, respect, and gentleness. It dawned on Sandy and me that we were providing two very nurturing, Christian environments and keeping Emily and Leeann away from the world. We had to ask ourselves, "Are we really preparing the girls for the real world they're going to have to live in someday?" The answer, arrived at after much prayer and thought, was, "No."

With God's guidance and heavy hearts we put the girls in

public middle school. Let me tell you, it hasn't been easy. The girls got hit in the face with the real world and it's not been pretty. Culture shock, pure and simple. Kids swearing, fighting, and cheating. Teachers with liberal agendas. No mention of Christ, unless it's someone using His name in vain. We've had to pull together as a family to give Emily and Leeann the needed support and encouragement.

The girls, to their credit, have adjusted and are doing well. Their faith is stronger, more muscular than before. What thrills Sandy and me is that they're standing up for Christ in a secular world. They didn't have to stand up for Christ in the Christian school. Just about everybody believed in Him. Now, they are the minority, and their faith is tested every day.

My Emily won't cheat, even though many of her fellow students do on a regular basis. Leeann is quiet in class and obedient to her teachers, even when many of her friends talk and are disruptive. Just about every female student in their school has seen the movie *Titanic* more than once. Emily and Leeann refuse to see it and don't mind saying so, because it contains nudity and foul language and glamorizes premarital sex. That's faith. A battle-tested faith that is growing and maturing because it's been exposed to the world.

I'm not suggesting all of you need to put your kids in public school. In fact, our Nancy still attends a Christian school. This move for Emily and Leeann was clearly what God wanted us to do. It has turned out to be the way we forced our girls to deal with the real world. There are other ways to do it. If your kids are in Christian schools, or if they're homeschooled, make sure you don't shelter them too much from the world's culture. The point is, you need to find ways to release your kids into the world. Do it while they're still in your home; that way you can guide and support them in the process.

If you truly want your kids to be like Jesus Christ, they must be in regular contact with the world. In John 17:6–18, Jesus reveals in His prayer that while He was not of the world, He was certainly in it. Jesus wants His disciples to go into the world and share the good news of His death and resurrection. I think our ultimate job as parents is summed up powerfully in the words of Jesus in John 17:18:

> *"As you sent me into the world,*
> *I have sent them into the world."*

Peel Yourself off Your Child

The solution for you overprotective parents is to gently, but firmly, peel yourself off your child. It will be like ripping duct tape off a hairy arm. It's going to hurt. And it will be hard on your kid. But it is necessary in order to launch him or her out into the world.

Face your own fears about life and resolve them. Allow your child more responsibility and freedom in life. Let your child experience pain and failure. That's the way we all learn how to live.

For instance, your son Johnny mentions his science project at the last minute. It's due tomorrow! He expects you to do what you've always done: rush around and take care of it for him. This time, you don't do that. This time, you let Johnny face the music.

You say to Johnny, "Son, you're on your own. I've done way too much of your schoolwork up to now, and that stops tonight. You're the one in school, not me. Do the best you can with the time you have. Look in the encyclopedia and surf the Net. Tomorrow you'll have to face your teacher—alone—and explain what happened. In the future, I'll be available to help you to a degree with your schoolwork. But only if you give me plenty of notice. Good night, son, and Godspeed. Live long and prosper!"

That thud is the sound of Johnny's jaw dropping on the floor. He'll whimper, beg, moan, threaten, pout, and be furious with you. Hold the line. He's got to learn to stand up on his own two legs and be a man. When Johnny screws up on his job as an adult, you won't be there to say: "Excuse me, Mr. Taylor, I'm Johnny's mom and I'd like to explain what happened the other day. . ." I don't think so. Johnny will be on his own some-day. Give him a good taste of independent living now.

THREE

If in Doubt, Wimp Out: The Permissive Parent

Don't Be Cruel to a Heart That's True

T he second parenting style is that of the permissive parent. You meekly submit to your child's whims, demands, and temper tantrums. You are upset by your child's anger and will do anything to stop it. Your child's anger frightens you and makes you feel out of control. Deep down, you fear the loss of your child's love. Chances are, you've been rejected in your life and you don't want to run the risk of losing a relationship with your child. You want peace and harmony at any price.

You can't stand a scene and your kid knows it. So she creates a scene whenever she wants something. You really can't blame her, can you? It works like a charm. When Susie screams for the box of candy in aisle five in the grocery store, Susie gets the candy. Susie isn't stupid. She waits until there's quite a crowd in aisle five: some retired persons, a policeman, and a child protection agency worker. Susie wouldn't waste her precious little breath screaming and whining in an empty aisle. She's learned she gets better results when there are spectators for her fits.

Kids are born with a sinful nature (Romans 3:23), and they want everything to go their way. They're convinced their parents' only reason for existence is to give them what they want. For example, when my Emily was two years old, she developed a very distinctive style of asking for her juice cup.

When she got thirsty and didn't know where her plastic sipper cup was (and she never knew where it was), she'd walk up to Sandy or me and say in a confident and even tone, "Cupper." Not, "Cupper, please." Just, "Cupper." If we didn't immediately spring into action, locate her cup, and make sure it was full of apple juice, Emily would begin screaming at the top of her lungs, "CUPPER, CUPPER, CUPPER!" She didn't care what we were doing at the time she asked for her cup. The Queen had spoken. She would stop screaming only when she had her cup and was guzzling juice down her selfish little throat.

Just to show that boys are as selfish as girls are, I'll tell you a story about my son, William. For a period of about six months when he was three, William came up with a unique way of expressing his displeasure with life. When he was unhappy and things weren't going his way, he'd march right up to Sandy and me. With his little hands on his hips and a big frown on his face, he'd say in a loud voice, "Make me happy!" Of course, we'd laugh out loud and he'd get even angrier. He really thought it was our job to make sure he was happy—twenty-four hours a day.

Look, kids are already selfish. Selfish to the core. You're adding to it! Permissiveness feeds selfishness.

Here Comes Santa Claus

You give gifts and privileges in the hope that the child will appreciate them, love you, and behave well. Once again, this is a complete misunderstanding of human nature. I mean, you're not even close!

Let me tell you about human nature. Christmastime, our

home, the early 1990s. We had the three girls: Emily, Leeann, and Nancy. William had not been born yet. My parents were in town. Now, you know what it means when grandparents are in town for Christmas. Unbelievable, obscene materialism. My folks backed up a huge U-Haul truck filled with presents. All for my kids, of course. When we got done unloading this massive cornucopia of giftdom, the only part of our Christmas tree still visible was the tiny blinking angel at the top.

When Christmas morning came, my girls were literally dancing with excitement and anticipation. Being a clinical psychologist, I decided to do a little research experiment. I timed the girls as they opened their gifts. It took them forty-five minutes to open all their presents. And they were moving fast. It took me a minute and a half to open my gifts: a couple of pairs of underwear and a tie. That's okay. I wasn't bitter.

Here's where it got interesting. When they finally finished opening their presents, my three girls came up to me in a little group and said something I will never forget: "Daddy, we are humbled by this outpouring of generosity. We simply cannot accept all these wonderful presents. After a brief prayer together, we've decided to give half of our presents to needy kids."

Is that what they said? Are you kidding? Of course not! What they really said was, "Where's the rest?" I couldn't believe it. I responded incredulously, "What do you mean, where's the rest? It took you forty-five minutes to open your gifts!" My girls were sure there were other presents for them hidden around the house. I said, "Not only are there no more presents for you, my dears, but we are going to give half of your presents to needy kids." I didn't actually say that last part, but I came close.

If you give and give and give to your kids, with no strings attached, their response will always be, "Where's the rest?" They'll never have enough.

No Rules, Just Nice

You permissive parents are unwilling to set rules and provide punishment when the rules are broken. You're too softhearted! When you do punish, you often give in and reduce the original punishment. You said, "You're grounded for one week, young man." And your son had earned the one-week grounding. But you lost your nerve. After just three days, you lifted the grounding. You wimp! You are not only losing respect, you are encouraging misbehavior.

You want to be your child's pal, his friend. You are not the authority figure you need to be. You are a parent, not a friend! Parenting is not a popularity contest. There will be many times you'll need to make extremely unpopular decisions and your kid will hate your guts. So be it. He'll get over it. He'll also respect you and learn some valuable lessons.

Have It Your Way

You have become a slave to your child's desires. Whatever your kid wants, your kid gets. Your kid is completely in control, and you're just along for the ride. You are loving and caring, but you're too weak. The message you're sending to your child is this: "You can have whatever you want, you can do whatever you want, and there will be no consequences."

Your child becomes progressively more demanding, selfish, and impulsive. She is not satisfied with what she has and always wants more. Her appetite is insatiable. She is the ultimate taker. Her motto is, "What have you done for me today?"

Your child believes she can act out in any way in the world and get away with it. Why? Because she always has! You're always there to cushion the blow. To soften the consequences. To clean up her mess. She never has to face the results of her actions, so she never learns from her mistakes. In fact, she learns to blame others for her own mistakes. Nothing is ever her fault.

She got that poor grade because the teacher was incompetent or didn't like her. She got that speeding ticket because that policeman had it in for her. She did pot because her friends pressured her. She skipped church because those other girls in the youth group were jealous of her and treated her badly. You are raising a liar, a manipulator, and a person who is unwilling to change and grow.

Spiritually, your spoiled child will see God the same way she sees you. He's nothing more than a supernatural Santa Claus who exists to meet her requests. Her relationship with God consists of a shopping list of her perceived needs. As long as God is coming through for her, she'll feel okay about Him. But when He disappoints her, she'll cut Him off. She'll blame Him for her unhappiness.

She learns to lack respect for others and their rights. In her humble opinion, she's the only one who has any rights. She has no tolerance for pain and disappointment. That's too bad, because life is full of it! She doesn't see pain as an opportunity to grow and build her faith in God. She sees it as a terrible, unnecessary intrusion into her life. She'll do anything to stop the pain and be happy again. She has no ability to work for rewards, or exercise self-discipline. She expects good things just to be handed to her on a silver platter.

If you want to get a clear view of how God feels about permissive parenting, read chapters 2, 3, and 4 of 1 Samuel. These chapters tell the sad story of Eli and his two sons, Hophni and Phinehas. Eli was a good and godly man. He was a judge, a priest, and the leader of Israel. But he was a permissive parent and that ended up being his legacy.

Eli's two sons were incredibly wicked. As priests, they should have been giving to the people and serving God faithfully. But they were selfish, arrogant men who wanted more and more power and possessions. They couldn't get enough. They had no love or respect for God. They had the gall to treat God's offerings in the temple with contempt.

Eli knew what his sons were doing. He was aware of all their sins. What did this great man of God do about it? Nothing. Nothing at all. In a classic, permissive parenting move, all he did was talk to them. He wrung his hands and told Hophni and Phinehas he didn't approve of their sinful behavior. But he took no action of any kind. As a result of his inaction, his sons were killed and many Israelites lost their lives.

This story powerfully communicates three truths. One, even a godly parent can be permissive. Two, the consequences for permissive parenting are severe. The children suffer, the parent suffers, and others suffer. Third, God is not pleased with permissive parenting. Read God's chilling words for Eli in 1 Samuel 3:13:

> *"For I told him that I would judge his family*
> *forever because of the sin he knew about;*
> *his sons made themselves contemptible,*
> *and he failed to restrain them."*

The story of Eli and his sons may seem like an extreme and exceptional case. It's not. I've seen many permissive parents and their kids whose situations were as serious, in their own way, as Eli and his sons. These kids, if pampered and spoiled, begin with tantrums. They move on to disrespect. They use cold, stony silence. They scream to get their way. Then they accuse their parents of abuse. They make all kinds of terrible threats. They physically abuse the parents who gave them life. Along the way, like Hophni and Phinehas, they ruin their lives and their parents' lives. I've seen it all, over and over. And all this happens because a parent won't draw a line in the sand and say, "No. No more. This far, and no farther."

Stop the Gravy Train

The solution for you permissive parents is to stop being the Sugarplum Fairy! Stop the Gravy Train. From an early age, make your kids earn rewards by the sweat of their brows. Don't work them to death, but make them work. Get tough and win back your children's respect. Without respect, there is no love. Your efforts to please your children and win their love actually end up destroying any chance for love. They won't just not love you. They'll hate you.

Set limits and apply consequences when the limits are broken. Children need limits, and it's your job as the parent to provide those limits. If you do, your kids will develop internal control and self-discipline. They'll create, with your help, an accurate and moral inner compass that will guide them in life. They'll respect you, honor you, and love you. If you've been permissive, this process won't be easy. It'll be a battle. But it's a battle you can win, and you must win.

When Susie throws a fit at home, ignore it. Step over her and go about your business. No emotion. No anger. No reaction. When Susie gets no response to her screaming and flopping around, she'll eventually quit. Kids throw tantrums only for attention, a reaction, and to get what they want.

If Susie is ornery enough and strong-willed enough, she'll hold her breath until she gets her way. Here's what you say: "Let's see how long Susie can hold her breath!" Make it a game. "Wow! That was thirty seconds, Susie! Great job! Let's go for a new record." If she actually passes out, no problem. Do you know what happens the instant she passes out? That's right. The brain kicks in and Susie's breathing resumes. She'll wake up with a small headache. She'll lose a few brain cells. Don't worry—she's got plenty.

If Susie chooses to have a fit in a public place—like aisle five in the grocery store—here's what you do. You lean down and say in a firm voice, "Susie, you have exactly ten seconds to stop your fit and be quiet. If you don't, I'm going to take you home to pay the piper." Susie will ask, "Who's the piper?" Then you'll say, "I'm the piper, Susie!" And you take her home and give her the discipline she so richly deserves.

FOUR

My Way or the Highway: The Authoritarian Parent

You rule your child with an iron fist. You make all the decisions. You are older. You are wiser. Therefore, you conclude, you know best. Plus, you have a deep need to be in control. You're not malicious about it. In fact, you believe orchestrating all the facets of your child's life is in his best interest. If he were allowed to make his own decisions, he'd make some bad ones. He might get hurt. He might make some moral mistakes. He might drift from God. No, you can't take these risks. You will single-handedly keep him on the right track every day by telling him exactly what to do. Exactly what to think. Exactly what to feel.

You control every aspect of your child's life. Nothing escapes your attention. You pick his hairstyle. You pick his friends. You pick his activities. You pick the posters and knickknacks he puts up in his room. You pick the clothes that are acceptable and those that are unacceptable.

Who died and made you king? Your kid can't make the slightest move on his own. When he wants to do anything, he must come to the throne room on bended knee. With eyes lowered in humility, he makes his plea. All he can hope is that his timing is right, and the king is in a decent mood. He prays that he can successfully answer his majesty's fifty questions about the proposed activity.

"I'm Right, So You're Wrong"

Your child is very careful not to voice an opinion in your presence, unless it is your opinion. He has learned the hard way that he is not allowed to disagree with you. Since you're always right, your child's opinion really isn't necessary. You are genuinely convinced that you have cornered the market on truth. When you open your mouth to speak, your child should listen and agree without question. The king, or queen, has spoken. It's your way or the highway!

My mother, Kathy, is a registered nurse. Like a lot of RNs (or "Royal Ninnies," as my dad would sometimes tease, making the three of us laugh uproariously), she is one tough cookie. A very bright and strong person who can handle just about any crisis in stride. My mom is a wonderful and loving person, but she did display one small parenting quirk as I was growing up.

Does the word *suppository* mean anything to you? If you're a squeamish person or have just eaten a meal, read the following story with caution. My mother, the RN, believed wholeheartedly in the power of suppository healing. A suppository is a small, missile-shaped object that is inserted into the body through a certain orifice. I'm not talking about the mouth. I think you get the picture.

For some strange reason (maybe it's an RN thing), my mother's answer to all my health problems as a kid was a suppository. Got the sniffles, David? I think you need a suppository. A head cold? A suppository. The flu? A suppository. An upset stomach? A suppository. A hacking cough? A suppository. A scraped knee? That's right, a suppository. Looking back, I think maybe she had bought a huge supply of suppositories on sale and had to get rid of them.

It was amazing how much better I suddenly felt when faced with a suppository. The cure was far, far worse than the disease. When I saw Mom walking down the hallway holding that dreaded missile in her gloved fingers, suddenly my pain was gone! "That's okay, Mom. I feel a lot better." There may have been a method to my mom's suppository madness. Those little medicinal jewels sure cut off the whining.

My mom was not an authoritarian parent, but this is an example of the kind of thinking found in authoritarian parents. She sincerely believed her way was the best way, and she wouldn't entertain other possible remedies. "How about a pill, or a lozenge, or a heating pad, Mom?" "No, David, I think a suppository is the answer." The Queen of Health had spoken. Fortunately for me, my mom was authoritarian only in this one area. A true authoritarian parent thinks this way in all areas.

Not only do you believe you're always right, authoritarian parent, you also cannot tolerate disagreement from your child. For you, disagreement is nothing short of a personal attack. And your response is swift and angry. You'll verbally belittle and shame your child and you won't even realize you're doing it. You're just regaining control.

Attila the Hun

In the area of discipline, you have all the subtlety of a wrecking ball. Your punishment for disobedience tends to be too harsh, even for minor infractions of the rules. You yell. You spank too hard. You ground the kid for a month for something small. You authoritarian parents are too heavy-handed. You're overkill tough. Way too hard-nosed. You think you're fair. You're not! You're Attila the Hun!

Your kids are afraid of you. When you come home, it's like a scene from an old Western. In every old Western worth its salt, there's one scene where the bad gunfighter rides into town on his bad horse. The good townsfolk see him coming and scatter. Women and children clear the streets. No one wants to take the chance of offending Dirty Jake and being humiliated. Or worse, cut down by a hail of bullets. Is this what happens when you come home from work?

The Bible is not silent on the topic of authoritarian parents. In fact, God has some pointed and helpful words for those of you who fall into this third parenting category. In two brief passages in the New Testament, both written by the apostle Paul, God reveals the damage authoritarianism causes in children and how to correct it.

These two verses, Ephesians 6:4 and Colossians 3:21, are addressed to fathers. But their message is also for mothers. Scripture clearly teaches that mothers are a vital part of the parenting process (Proverbs 1:8; 6:20).

Fathers, do not exasperate your children;
instead, bring them up in the training
and instruction of the Lord.
EPHESIANS 6:4

Fathers, do not embitter your children,
or they will become discouraged.
COLOSSIANS 3:21

"Exasperate" and "embitter." Powerful words that vividly describe what happens inside the child of an authoritarian parent. Paul is saying, in a very direct way, do not be too hard on your children. Don't be harsh. Don't make unreasonable demands. Don't provoke, irritate, or agitate. These authoritarian actions will damage your children. They'll become angry or discouraged.

Whenever God admonishes, He also provides the way out. He gives the solution to the problem. For authoritarian parents, the answer is found in the final clause of Ephesians 6:4: "Instead, bring them up in the training and instruction of the Lord." The language Paul uses here paints a picture of parents who nourish their children and meet their needs. Parents who train and instruct their precious children using the Lord's principles. God wants us to parent our children as He parents us: with firmness and love.

I saw a family in therapy that illustrated what God is talking about in these two passages. It was a family of four: Dad, Mom, and two teenage sons. I knew I had an industrial-strength authoritarian parent on my hands thirty seconds into the first session. Dad was a big, burly man with a foghorn voice and the bearing of General George C. Patton. His two sons were treated like buck privates in his own private army.

General Patton told his privates where to sit and how to sit. He told them what to say and how to say it. He interrupted them continually to correct them and set them straight on their facts. He made it painfully clear how disappointed he was with their behavior. He even browbeat them with Scripture. His mousy wife stayed quiet, her body folded into a defensive, protective posture.

One son was angry at his father. He was acting out to show

Dad he couldn't be controlled. The other son was deeply discouraged. He was quiet, passive, and withdrawn. A yes-man. A young man who reminded me of a dependent, broken, and whipped dog. Were these boys exasperated by their father? No doubt. Embittered? You'd better believe it.

Could I do anything about it? Not a chance. This dad was in complete control and wanted to stay that way. Even at the price of losing both his sons. I tried to get through to him, but he didn't want to hear what I had to say.

He was actually a decent, well-meaning man. He didn't realize his kids experienced his parenting style as a reign of terror. Privately, I told him he was authoritarian and that his kids were being damaged. He didn't believe me. He was offended by my comments and ended the therapy. He marched his wife and kids to the car and drove off in a cloud of dust.

As a clinical psychologist, I've seen many authoritarian parents and their children. Some parents, like this man, never get it. They refuse to get it. They won't relinquish control. Some do see what they're doing and learn to back off. What choice will you make?

Don't Think, Just Obey

Being authoritarian doesn't make you a bad person. It doesn't even make you a bad parent. It's just your tendency. Your weakness. You probably had an authoritarian parent growing up, and so it's a learned habit. But it's a style you need to change. The message you're sending to your child, day in and day out, is this: "You aren't able to think for yourself, so you must follow the rules of others."

Spontaneity and creativity are crushed in your child. Any

form of independent thinking or self-expression is punished, so it doesn't develop. Your child feels unloved and stupid. This is the last thing you want, but it's what happens. Inside your child, tremendous resentment builds up against parents and all authority figures. This seething resentment will cripple your child, because we all must answer to authority in our lives: the police, the courts, the boss, the wife. (Just kidding about that last one.)

Your child will resist supervision and instruction from those in positions of leadership. She'll struggle with teachers, employers, and even the pastors and elders in the church. And, ultimately, of course, it is God whom we need to obey, and whose guidance we must follow by means of the Bible and the Holy Spirit. But your child won't. She'll fight an internal war with God and be unwilling to submit to Him. Without realizing it, you've taught her to reject any type of submission on her part. The irony is, a child so focused on being her own person and answering to no one will have great difficulty achieving independence. She just doesn't know how.

Back in my college days, Sandy and I had a number of friends from very strict homes. All the way through high school, they were allowed no freedom. They were kept on a short leash. They really didn't know how to think for themselves. Their parents did not risk giving their teenagers the freedom of making some decisions on their own and learning the wisdom of following loving admonitions and instructions. Their parents did all the thinking and their kids simply had to obey.

Guess what happened when these Christian kids hit college, and Mom and Dad weren't around anymore? That's right. They finally had freedom, and they couldn't handle it. These kids went crazy. They drank, smoked, partied all night, and acted in incredibly irresponsible ways. They made all kinds of moral and spiritual mistakes. Worst of all, they questioned their faith and drifted far from God. Their parents had not prepared them for the wide-open freedom of college. They literally crashed and burned.

Lighten Up!

What's the solution for you authoritarian parents? Give up your need to control. Find out what drives this need and fix it. Learn to laugh and play with your child. For heaven's sake—and your kid's sake—lighten up! Be a person, not an ogre. Develop some tenderness and compassion for your children. Come down from your perch on Mount Olympus and get to know your children. They're really neat and interesting persons.

Now comes the really tough part. Allow your child to make decisions on her own. Allow her to express her personal feelings and thoughts and opinions. Allow her to disagree with you! By allowing these forms of personal expression, you will enable your child to learn how to think.

The next time your son is saying something you don't agree with, fight the urge to cut him off. Choke back your desire to set him straight in your usual overbearing, take-no-prisoners way. Let him talk and express himself. You don't have to agree, but just listen and give him time to have the floor. You'll get your chance, when he's done, to firmly and gently share your view. The relationship you're building with your son or daughter is infinitely more important than whatever issue is being discussed. Isn't it?

FIVE

The Human Mistake Detector: The Perfectionist Parent

Kids Will Be Kids

Life is never dull with kids. It's also never peaceful, orderly, or predictable. Here are just a few snapshots from my checkered parenting career.

Diapers and I never got along. I can't count the times I had to fight to put a diaper on a squirming, screaming, writhing kid. It was like roping a calf and tying its legs together. And often—shockingly often—just at the instant I had finally attached the diaper, I heard an explosion. I looked down to see a tiny smirk on the kid's face. Great! Another cleanup job, and another whole new steel-cage diaper wrestling match.

One night—no, actually, it was early in the morning—Sandy and I were awakened by the cries of two-week-old Nancy in her cradle at the foot of our bed. Sandy gave me a look that said, "Don't even think about it. This time, you're changing her." Barely awake, I stumbled to the cradle and put Nancy on the bed. In the dim light of my clock radio, I cleaned her up and slid the new diaper into place. As I leaned in close to see what I was doing, I heard a funny squirting noise. A split second later, I was hit smack in the face with a stream of human waste. And it wasn't "Number One." The most humiliating part was having to endure Sandy's hysterical laughter.

My diaper troubles are not the only examples of pain and suffering my kids have inflicted upon me over the years. I had a wonderful adventure in the sky with my three lovely, sweet little girls a few years ago. Sandy, the three girls, and I were flying to California to visit my in-laws for Christmas. A non-stop flight from Tampa to Los Angeles with three young kids was a recipe for extreme pain. This trip was more traumatic than any of those made-for-television airplane disaster movies.

We were cruising along at 33,000 feet when the girls decided to erupt simultaneously into three screaming fits. They yelled, whined, and cried at the top of their lungs. Sandy and I tried everything—food, drink, diaper changes, holding them—but nothing worked. I was trapped in a long tube five miles from the ground with my out-of-control kids and a planeload of people who hated me. The old lady sitting in front of me turned and said to me through clenched teeth, "Young man, your children's behavior is disgraceful. Why, in my day, children were never allowed to act this way."

At this point, I wanted that plane to crash. I really did. I closed my eyes and created a fantasy about what it would be like if we did crash. First and foremost, I would be released from my torment. Also, as the plane hurtled toward earth, the passengers would completely forget about my kids. They wouldn't be able to hear my kids over their own screams. I would lean forward and say to the old lady, "Please be quiet, ma'am. Your pathetic screams are upsetting my children. Why, in my day, people had the decency to go to their fiery deaths in dignity."

My point with these stories is: Kids aren't perfect. They're learning how to live and they make a lot of mistakes along the way. Life with them is a wild ride filled with mayhem, mishaps, and misadventures of all kinds. Kids will be kids.

The perfectionist parents among us, following parenting style Number Four, don't seem to realize this, though. You see no excuse for immaturity and mistakes in your children. You really believe parenting ought to be a peaceful, orderly process that produces kids who act like adults. You don't like surprises. You hate it when your kids disrupt your prim and proper world. You dedicate yourself to teaching your kids how to be like you—perfect.

Inspector #9

I bought a new pair of slacks the other day at a classy men's store. I found a little white piece of paper in one of the pockets. On the paper was a brief message: "Inspected by #9." I was comforted by the note, because it meant my slacks had passed a meticulous inspection by a person named #9. Inspector #9 had checked and rechecked every stitch, every square inch of my slacks and pronounced them fit for sale.

This careful inspection process is a great idea for slacks and other articles of clothing. It is not a great idea for kids. When you have a perfectionist parent, it's like living with Inspector #9. Everything you do, everything you say, and every move you make is inspected. Kids do not find this constant inspection comforting. They find it stressful, pressure-filled, and frustrating. They cringe every time a mistake is pointed out. And their parental inspectors point out a lot of mistakes. I mean, after all, isn't that the job of inspectors?

You perfectionist parents set impossibly high standards and accept your child only when these standards are met. You want your child's room cleaned to perfection. You're a fanatic about the kid's room! The white glove test isn't a joke in your home. Oh, no. You have a white glove and you use it. You are deeply offended by a messy room. To you, it's not just a messy room. It's a sign of a serious problem in your child's mind. It reveals a shockingly high level of irresponsibility and instability. A messy room is the first tragic step in your child's journey to becoming a criminal.

You want the underwear folded a certain way. No one ever sees underwear. Who cares how you fold it? You care. You want the lawn mowed to your precise specifications. You've done a topographical survey and you know just how it needs to be done. You want all the lights turned out when the child leaves a room—even if she's coming right back.

You are driving your children crazy! You think your standards are reasonable. They are not! You say you just want excellence. But there's a difference between excellence and perfection. You don't know the difference. Every day, you preach to your children that there is a right way and a wrong way to do everything. Of course, your way is the right way.

Criticism Comes First

You focus on the negative and ignore the positive. Your son, Bobby, washes the car. When he's done, you come out to check his work. The first thing out of your mouth is, "Bobby, you missed a spot here by the rear bumper. Look at that dirt! And, hey, the grill is covered with bug stains. Son, if you're going to do a job, you need to do it right." You don't seem to notice that most of the car is clean! You also don't seem to notice that you are stripping Bobby's self-esteem. The kid is eight years old! Give him a break, will you?

Your daughter, Sharon, is walking down the hall toward you holding her report card. She's literally shaking as she takes this long, lonely walk. For her, it's like walking to the gas chamber. She knows exactly what you're going to do. She hands the report card to you and flinches as she prepares for the inevitable. Her report card shows all A's and one B. What's the first thing out of your mouth? "Sharon, what's this B in math? Young lady, we got you a tutor. Didn't you study? I never got a B in math, I can tell you that. Good grades come from hard work. Why, when I was your age. . ."

You have failed to notice that Sharon has handed you an excellent report card. All A's and one B? That's pretty good, wouldn't you say? No, you wouldn't. Because as a perfectionist, all you notice is the B. Your mind, and your tongue, zero in on mistakes, weaknesses, and any behavior that falls short of your lofty standards. When your child does produce superior behavior that meets with your approval, you say nothing. This kind of excellence is just expected. You shouldn't have to pat a kid on the back for what she ought to be doing, right? Wrong!

Never Good Enough

You are impossible to please. You feel compelled to point out even minor, trivial mistakes. You just can't help yourself. If there's a piece of lint on your son's sweater, you'll mention it. If one strand of your daughter's hair is off-center, she'll hear about it. If your son missed one tiny spot under the toilet rim with the cleaning brush, you'll march him to the bathroom and show him his heinous mistake. If your daughter left a few crumbs on the kitchen counter, she'll be treated to a lecture on how she's putting her whole family at risk for food poisoning.

You perfectionist parents are focused on results, not effort. You are the parental equivalent of Vince Lombardi, the late, great football coach of the Green Bay Packers. For you and Vince, doing your best isn't good enough. Winning is all that counts. Your love is conditional. Your children must perform up to your expectations to win any kind of acceptance from you. Here is the message you are sending to your kids: "You must do everything perfectly."

Let me tell you what happens to your child, perfectionist parent. He becomes preoccupied with his performance, not his character. He feels inadequate and unworthy. He believes that because he is unable to please you—a tremendously significant and influential person in his life—there's something wrong with him. He's not smart enough. Not quick enough. Not dedicated enough. He believes he is never good enough in any area.

If I've heard the statement, "I was never good enough" once, I've heard it 50,000 times in my therapy office from adult clients. When a child cannot please a parent, she assumes she isn't good enough to please anyone else. If you allow your child to leave your home with this "never good enough" message stamped on her brain, she'll apply it to every relationship in her life as an adult.

She'll think she's never good enough as a friend. Never good enough as an employee. Never good enough as a wife. Never good enough as a mom. Never good enough as a child of God. Yes, her spiritual life and walk with God will be affected. She'll feel like she is unworthy of His time and attention. She'll feel like she can't really please Him. She'll try to earn His love just as she tried to earn yours. She won't be able to relax and just drink in His unconditional love and grace.

Your child will take one of two roads out of childhood.

One possibility is she'll become a perfectionist like you. Please. Spare the rest of us. We have enough perfectionists already. The other possibility is she'll give up and stop trying. Frustrated time and time again in her efforts to reach your standards, she'll quit and never reach her full potential.

It's the kids in this second category that I typically see in therapy. The picture is always the same. A bright kid in a good, solid family who is lazy and unmotivated. His grades and achievement in extracurricular activities do not come close to his ability level. His teachers, coaches, and other adults all say the same thing: "David is not achieving his potential." As I talk with David, I discover an insecure, scared kid who is afraid to take risks. He's afraid to really apply himself and do his best.

Why? Not always—but in many cases—the why is a perfectionist parent. David has tried and tried and tried to measure up to his perfectionist parent, but he has failed. He is deeply discouraged. He has realized he'll never please you, so he's quit trying. So, he settles for being a semi-failure who, for some unknown reason, isn't achieving his full potential. This middle ground position gives him at least some control and comfort.

Bite Your Tongue and Be Positive

As usual, the parent is the key to motivating David to leave the safety of his laziness. My job is to convince the perfectionist parent to change her parenting style. The solution for David's parents, and for all perfectionist parents, is to lower your standards to a reasonable level.

The truth is, though, you wouldn't know a reasonable

level if it came up and smacked you in the face. So, you'll have to humble yourself and ask your spouse for help with your standards. Or ask a close friend, your pastor, or a Christian counselor. It won't be easy to swallow your pride and ask for assistance, but you can do it. You'd better do it—for your kid's sake.

Praise your child for effort and personal qualities. Look for the positive and reinforce it on a daily basis. Praise is one of the main ways parents build character and self-esteem. Praise is a powerful motivator for a child. There are times when you need to correct and use constructive criticism, but there ought to be many more times when you praise. So stop expecting good behavior and then letting it pass without comment. Start praising your child for every behavior you appreciate. Let the healing begin.

Learn to relax and not be so obsessed with getting every little job done around the house. You spend all your time doing your jobs and trying to get your kid to do his jobs. Each job is critically important and must be done your way and in your time frame. Let some jobs go and enjoy life! In your mad rush to accomplish all these daily tasks, you are missing your child. You're very productive. We have to give you that. But you're missing opportunity after opportunity to connect with your kid and build the relationship. What's more important? Getting the dishes done right after dinner, or playing a game with your daughter? Putting the last load of laundry in the washer, or throwing the football with your son?

Notice how Jesus Christ handled a perfectionist. In Luke 10:38–42, Jesus visited the home of a woman named Martha. When Jesus arrived, Martha's sister, Mary, sat at His feet listening to Him talk. Martha was busy rushing around the house making sure everything was just right for her special guest. She resented doing all the work by herself, so she went to Jesus and complained about Mary not helping her. Jesus' reply to Martha in Luke 10:41–42 is a healthy message for all perfectionists:

> *"Martha, Martha," the Lord answered,*
> *"you are worried and upset about many things,*
> *but only one thing is needed.*
> *Mary has chosen what is better,*
> *and it will not be taken away from her."*

All you Marthas—male and female—need to get your priorities straight. The jobs can wait. Your relationship with your child cannot.

Finally, perfectionist parents, stop being a human mistake detector. Get it through your thick skulls that kids can't be perfect! Give up trying to make them perfect. Keep your mouth shut after small mistakes. For instance, say it's a weekday morning and you're on the couch reading the newspaper. Your daughter Jackie is walking by on her way to school. You lower the paper and notice that one of her hair clips is just a little out of place. Here's the challenge of a lifetime for you: Say nothing. Bite your tongue.

The sheer effort it takes to choke back what you desperately want to say will cause you to shake, rock back and forth on the couch, and make funny little noises. Jackie will notice that you seem to be having some kind of seizure, and she'll turn and ask, "Mom, what's the matter?" You'll just have to wave her off and hang on for dear life. After she's left the house and is out of earshot, you can scream to the empty house,

"One of her hair clips is not in the right place!"

Now, if your kid's walking out the door with the fly on his pants down, say something. "Hey, your zipper's down. Feel the breeze? Zip it up." If you notice a big mustard stain on your daughter's blouse, you can point that out too. Or if your son is coming out of the bathroom and he's dragging the toilet paper roll because it stuck to his shoe, feel free to let him know. But if it's something small and insignificant. . .just shut up!

SIX

Can't You See I'm Busy?
The Uninvolved Parent

Who Is Your Opus?

If you want to see a great movie with a profound message, rent *Mr. Holland's Opus*. Even though there are no gunfights or exploding cars, it's a classic. Richard Dreyfuss plays Glenn Holland, a young composer. As the movie begins, Glenn is newly married and in need of a job. His one great dream is to write a brilliant symphony. He fervently believes that completing his opus will be the crowning achievement of his life. It's what he was born to do. Unfortunately, an incomplete opus doesn't pay the bills. So Glenn reluctantly takes a job as the music teacher at John F. Kennedy High School.

At first, he hates the job. He despises the job. Teaching music to a bunch of unmotivated, ungrateful teenage punks is his worst nightmare. He sees his teaching as a necessary, and very temporary, evil. Its only purpose is to allow him to continue working on his symphony. He teaches during the day, and then rushes home to spend hours composing his opus.

But as the years go by at John F. Kennedy High School, a strange thing happens. Glenn Holland begins to enjoy his teaching. He finds satisfaction in exposing kids to music and helping them learn to play the instruments. He develops an uncanny ability to connect with his students and create real changes in their lives. Without even realizing it, he becomes a master teacher.

Glenn himself can't yet see the tremendous value of his teaching. As he ages, he continues to work on his opus in the little spare time he can find. He still considers his opus the focal point of his life. The one thing dearest to his heart. The reason for his existence. He becomes deeply discouraged because he can't finish his symphony. He wonders if anyone will ever hear it besides him and his long-suffering wife.

Near the end of the movie, the smarmy principal terminates Glenn's job because of budget cuts. On his last day at school, sixty-year-old Glenn cleans out his classroom and prepares to leave. He feels like a complete failure. He, his wife, and son walk by the auditorium and hear noise. They walk to the door and open it. Glenn is shocked to see the auditorium packed with hundreds of his former students. It's a huge surprise party for him in honor of his thirty years as music teacher.

He walks to the front, greeting along the way students whose lives he has impacted over the years. The governor of the state, a former student, gives a brief speech in which she thanks Mr. Holland for his years of dedicated service. She tells him everyone knows he's been working on his symphony for the last thirty years. She says she knows he feels like he's wasted his life because his precious opus has never been performed. Then she tells him that he is, in fact, a tremendous success. "Look around this auditorium," she says. "We are your symphony, Mr. Holland. We are the notes and the melodies of your life."

Powerful stuff. If you don't cry at the end of this movie you're not human. (You are a world-class "clam," and you need to read my book, *Men Are Clams, Women Are Crowbars,* published by Barbour Publishing.) The point of the movie is that

Glenn Holland was meant to be a teacher, not a composer. He was a fantastic teacher. That was his passion. That was his life. He was also a composer. That's true. But his composing was secondary. It blinded him from seeing that his real value was in another, far less glamorous area.

Many parents, like Glenn Holland, are blinded and can't see their real purpose in life. They don't realize the incredible value and importance of raising their children. Parenting is a nuisance, a bother, and certainly far from a priority. Parenting gets in the way of what they really want to do in their lives. You know: the important things like career, money, fame, friends, and hobbies.

These parents just don't get it. They somehow miss God's message that being a parent is one of the most important jobs on earth. Nurturing and loving and teaching and raising your kids is second in priority only to building and maintaining a great marriage. God has given parents the awesome responsibility of shaping and molding persons to be like Him. Parenting ought to be your great dream. Your passion. Your life's work. Your kids are your opus!

Giving Your Kids the Leftovers

Regrettably, you uninvolved parents are the parents who don't get it. Your kids are not your opus. Everything and everybody else is your opus. You are not home much, so you give very little time and attention to your children. You may be a workaholic, driven to succeed in your career. You get to work early and you come home late. Day after day after day.

You may have an overdeveloped social life. Your friends mean a great deal to you. You'd rather be with them than with your own kids. You participate in too many activities outside the home. You golf on the weekends. You take frequent hunting and fishing trips. You're overloaded with church activities. Every time they open the church door, you're there doing something for someone. Your commitment to physical fitness is impressive. You spend hours each week at the gym, toning and firming your beautiful body.

Your personal life is the priority, and your kids get the leftovers. The things you want to do come first. Is it such a crime to want to be happy, successful, and enjoy life? Actually, it is, if you end up neglecting your kids. You don't mean to neglect them. You may not even realize you neglect them. But most of your energy and passion goes to your personal pursuits. Whatever time is still there after you've satisfied yourself is offered to the kids. You can't say no to your job, your friends, or your activities. You can, however, say no to your kids. You're good at that. You do it all the time.

Home, but Not Home

Even when you are home, you're not really home. You stay in your own personal zone. You don't play with your kids. You don't talk to your kids. You don't interact with your kids in any meaningful way. You're wrapped up in your own stuff! You piddle in the garage. You watch television. You read the paper. You talk on the phone. You tippy, tappy, tippy on the computer keyboard as you send e-mails and surf the Net.

Your kids ask you to play, but you brush them off:

• "Not now, honey."
• "I'm too tired."

- "I just want to relax."
- "Can't you see I'm busy?"
- "I had a hard day."
- "Maybe another time."

Pretty soon, the kids give up and don't even bother asking anymore. Oh, you're home all night. You're in the building. But you might as well be gone, for all the good your presence is doing your kids.

You miss special events like birthdays, baseball games, and school presentations. Your kid looks for you, but you're not there. Do you have any idea how important it is to your child to see you in the audience at a school program or a sporting event? Do you realize your excuses don't fool your child? Don't you remember, back when you were a kid, the intense feeling of pride and warmth you got inside as you saw your mom and dad sitting there? Maybe your parents weren't there, and you know how that felt. Maybe you don't know the good feelings. Just trust me. Those feelings are enormously significant to a kid. When you don't show up, your child gets these intense feelings inside: disappointment, rejection, and loneliness. This is what kids tell me in my office—and I believe them.

You uninvolved parents are being selfish. You don't mean to be. You're not aware that you spend most of your free time meeting your own needs. You're not maliciously trying to hurt your kids. But you are selfish, and you are hurting your kids. If you didn't have kids, it wouldn't make any difference. But you do have kids and they need you! They need your time. They need your attention. They need to be taught things that only you can teach them.

You are missing the chance to build a relationship with your children. It's going to cost them and it's going to cost you. One of the joys of adult children is having a good, close relationship with them. You can be great friends! You can have a terrific time together talking, laughing, eating, going out, and sharing each other's lives. You uninvolved parents won't have a relationship like this with your adult kids. They'll ignore you. They'll feel awkward around you. They'll tolerate you. Why? Because they don't know you.

Believe me, uninvolved parents, I'm not throwing stones. I have been where you are now. It is so easy to be an uninvolved parent and not even know you are one. Life can be so incredibly busy that you allow your priorities to get out of whack. Early in my career as a psychologist, I spent long hours building my practice. I was seeing clients, developing talks, speaking, meeting with pastors and other Christian leaders, and doing a million and one things to get established in the Tampa Bay community.

I wasn't home much. When I was home, I was still thinking about my career and how to improve it. Frankly, I was obsessed with building my practice and becoming successful. Sandy and our two young daughters, Emily and Leeann, were getting the short end of the stick. The crazy part was, I didn't think I was too busy. I didn't think for a minute that I was an uninvolved parent. I was even giving parenting workshops and telling other moms and dads to spend time with their kids. I really thought I was doing fine as a dad. I was wrong.

Sandy's patience finally wore thin and she confronted me with my workaholism and lack of real time with the family. I tried that classic workaholic line on her: "But I'm working for you and the kids!" Sandy said: "Baloney, buddy. You're working for yourself, and you've gotten carried away." And then she said the words that got my attention: "We don't need more money. We don't need a successful psychologist and speaker. We need you."

I have worked hard these last seven or eight years to change. To spend good quantity, as well as quality, time with each of my kids. To be involved in their lives. I'm still busy, but I control my schedule now, and not the other way around. Sandy and I have a deal. If she tells me I'm too busy, I'm too busy. She and the four kids define my involvement as a dad. I don't define it. If any one of the five of them says I need to be home more, I accept it and make adjustments.

The Parent and the Pool

I hate my pool. Words cannot adequately express the deep, passionate loathing I carry in my gut for my pool. No one warned me what owning a pool would actually be like. The salesman gushed on and on about all the fabulous advantages of a pool. Clean, fresh, cool, sparkling water. Barbecues at poolside. Gracious parties on the deck. An extra ten thousand dollars when I sold my home. And so easy to maintain. Lies! All lies! If I could find that crummy salesman, I'd shoot him. Or better yet, drown him in my pool.

The reality is, I spend every day of my miserable life working on my pool. I fight a never-ending battle against a pool owner's worst enemy: algae. Green algae, yellow algae, black algae, plaid algae, and a hundred other varieties of algae—I have met them all. My dear wife Sandy will not allow a screen to be placed over the pool. She wants the pool to be exposed to the air and sun. It's easy for her to have no screen. I'm the poor slob that has to deal with the consequences of an open-air pool.

Everything God created ends up in my pool. Thousands of leaves from the two huge oak trees next door. Dirt. Bird droppings. Dead frogs. Snakes. Hair balls. Sticks. Branches. Bugs of all kinds. Rocks. Meteors. Pieces of wreckage from satellites in space. And, from what I can tell, every single thing that touches my pool causes algae.

But the nastiest and most obnoxious pool invaders are the spores. The oak tree spores. Do you know what a spore is? It's a slimy, wormlike, two-inch long, brown piece of crusted reproductive matter that oak trees release by the millions every spring. Their spores fill my pool for two nightmarish months each year. They choke my skimmer basket and foul my pump. They spawn, not new oak trees, but algae. Lots and lots of algae. I will spend two hours cleaning out the spores and getting my pool in tip-top shape. As I stand back to admire the pristine water, a gust of wind shakes the oak trees. I can only watch in horror as thousands of spores slowly float down into my pool. "No, no, no!" I scream.

Boy, I feel better now. It helps to vent. But my real point is that maintaining my pool is a lot like parenting. I have found that I need to clean my pool every single day. I go out and check the chemical levels, add chemicals as needed, and clean out any debris in the pool. If I clean it daily, I can keep on top of things and the water stays clear and algae-free. But if I ignore it for even a few days, disaster strikes! It takes me hours, sometimes days, to bring the water back to a pure state.

It's the same way with kids. They need your time and attention and involvement every day. If you give them this daily dose of parental involvement, they will flourish and be healthy. But if you neglect your kids, bad things will happen. And it doesn't take long. (The rewards, however, of staying on top of things are even better with kids than with a pool.)

I'm Not O.K., You're Not O.K.

If you're an uninvolved parent, here's the message you're sending to your child: "You and the things you do are unimportant." It's a particularly devastating message. Your child will develop critically low self-esteem. No ifs, ands, or maybes about it. He will. Your child will conclude: "If my own parent thinks I'm unimportant, I must be." Exactly.

Your child will have difficulty forming close, warm relationships. A child learns how to build a relationship from the relationship his parent builds with him. So, if you don't build a relationship with your child, he won't know how to do it with anyone else. Some of you parents are thinking, "But, Dave, I'm not very good at relationships myself. I don't know how to build them." My friend, you need to learn how and you need to learn fast. Get help. The good news is, you can be taught. See a competent Christian psychologist and get started.

The child of an uninvolved parent will experience social problems, anxiety, and loneliness well into adulthood. A deep-seated insecurity will characterize her life. She won't feel connected to herself, others, or God. I'd be happy to see your adult child in therapy to work on these problems. I see many adult children of uninvolved parents and therapy does help them heal and become confident, secure individuals. But it is a difficult, painful, and expensive process. It would be better to make adjustments in your parenting now, so they can avoid seeing me.

When You Sit Down, Walk, Lie Down, and Get Up

The solution, as always, is in the Bible. Look at the parenting style described in Deuteronomy 6:5–7:

> *Love the LORD your God with all your heart*
> *and with all your soul and with all your strength.*
> *These commandments that I give you today*
> *are to be upon your hearts.*
> *Impress them on your children.*
> *Talk about them when you sit at home*
> *and when you walk along the road,*
> *when you lie down and when you get up.*

It's very important to God that parents teach His commandments to their children. This passage makes it clear that to be effective teachers, parents must have a close, personal, involved parenting style. Question: How can you teach your kids when you sit down, walk, lie down, and get up? Answer: By spending as much time as possible with your kids.

The key for you uninvolved parents is to make time for each child on a regular basis. I know you're busy. So am I. I maintain a full-time private practice, speak a great deal, write books, teach seminary classes, and take care of my pool. But I have learned to make time for my wife and my four kids. If I can do it, you can do it. And by the way, do what your child wants to do in your time together. That communicates love and will virtually guarantee a positive, enjoyable time.

Cut back your busy and important schedule. You may not be as successful, but it's worth the price. God says your job as a parent is more important to Him than being a big success in the eyes of the world. I've never heard these words yet from a child in my therapy office: "Yeah, my parents don't spend much time with me. But they're really successful and make a lot of money and that means more to me." These are the words I hear day in and day out from kids of all ages: "My folks are so busy! They don't play with me or talk with me very much. That makes me sad. I'd give anything to spend more time with them."

I was blessed to have two parents who were deeply and intimately involved in my life. My mom was home when I got home from school. My dad carved out time every Saturday morning just for me. For years, we went to the donut shop and then played tennis. Each evening during the week, we would talk and play games as a family. My mom and dad came to just about every athletic game I had: soccer, baseball, and football. All this time invested in me made me feel confident, secure, and loved. It also built a strong, close relationship with my parents—a relationship that has continued to get deeper in my adult years.

It is not acceptable to have a poor, distant relationship with a child. Keep trying to build a good one! Never give up! This is your responsibility as the adult. Once children leave home, they're gone. It's very difficult to build a relationship with them when they're adults and on their own. It's too late. You will never again have the day-to-day opportunities to build the relationship. Do it now, because now is all you've got.

Give Me That Good Old Agape: The Balanced Parent

You're thinking: Okay, you've covered all the parenting styles that are bad for my kids. I fit into almost every category! My poor kids don't have a chance! I can be overprotective. I've been permissive. I know at times I've gotten authoritarian. Can I help it if perfectionism runs in my family? I can get so busy some weeks that I'm sure I've slipped into the uninvolved mode. Look, I'll work on adjusting my dysfunctional parenting styles. Really, I will. But surely you can offer some positive alternative. Aren't there any good parenting styles? Please give me some hope.

Actually there is one parenting style I haven't mentioned yet. It's a good one. It's a healthy one. It's the one you want to have. It's the one God wants you to have. It's the balanced parent style. This is the style God the Father uses to parent us, His children.

God Is My Daddy

God loves us with an unconditional love. An agape love. A love that gives and gives and gives, with no expectation of anything in return. No strings attached.

> *This is love: not that we loved God,*
> *but that he loved us and sent his Son*

as an atoning sacrifice for our sins.
1 JOHN 4:10

What a love! God sent Jesus Christ to die for us, with no guarantee we would accept this sacrifice. We did nothing to deserve it. God gave the supreme gift, His Son's life, for one reason and one reason only: because He loves us.

Agape love is concerned only with the one loved. It is absolutely and utterly unselfish. No one has ever done a better job describing agape love than the apostle Paul in 1 Corinthians 13:4–7:

Love is patient, love is kind.
It does not envy, it does not boast, it is not proud.
It is not rude, it is not self-seeking,
it is not easily angered, it keeps no record of wrongs.
Love does not delight in evil but rejoices with the truth.
It always protects, always trusts,
always hopes, always perseveres.

Don't think, though, that God's agape love is a wimpy, wipe-your-feet-on-me kind of love. Not at all. It is a love that comes with clear limits. God is an incredibly gracious, loving Father, but He " 'disciplines those he loves, and he punishes everyone he accepts as a son' " (Hebrews 12:6). Proverbs 13:24 says: "He who spares the rod hates his son, but he who loves him is careful to discipline him." If we step out of line, God will get our attention. His punishment is an expression of His love. Its purpose is to teach, build character, and restore us to a close relationship with Him.

Limits with Love

Now, I don't know about you, but I can't think of a better example to follow as a parent than God. I want to parent my kids just like God parents me. Don't you? To parent God's way, you need to be the balanced parent. Like God, you strike a balance between love and limits.

You love your kids with an unselfish, unconditional love. You say the words "I love you" often. You make time. You build healthy relationships with each of your children. You meet needs. You also establish clear limits in your home. You set reasonable standards of behavior and apply reasonable rewards and consequences. When your kids choose to step outside your limits, they experience the pain of appropriate discipline.

Catch Me in the Act

As a balanced parent, you never assume you're doing everything right. In fact, you assume you're making some mistakes. You get regular feedback—from your spouse and from your kids. Their input helps you make the frequent adjustments necessary in the life of a good parent.

You build a marriage in which you invite your partner to tell you when you're doing your unhealthy parenting style. It's hard to catch yourself! I need Sandy to catch me doing my style, and I need to catch her doing hers. Of course, don't bring it up in front of the kids: "Dave, you wimp! You're being permissive again! Nancy needs to go to bed now." Tell your partner in private. If you're not married, get a close friend or family member to catch you in your dysfunctional style.

Involve your children in the parenting process. Value their feelings and opinions about the job you're doing as a parent.

On a regular basis, every two or three weeks, you ask your children these questions:

- "How am I doing as a parent?"
- "How can I do better as a mom (or dad)?"
- "What do you need from me?"

If you don't ask, they won't tell you. If you do ask, you'll get information crucial to your success as a parent. How can you accurately evaluate your parenting without input from those you are parenting? You can't! Plus, when you ask, your kids feel important and genuinely loved.

"I Love You, Man!"

The message balanced parents send to their children is: "You are loved and have the freedom to become who you are within limits." This is the healthiest and most godly message a parent can send. The impact on your kids is all positive. Your children will grow up emotionally and spiritually healthy. They'll have good self-esteem. Not worldly self-esteem, but Christ-centered self-esteem. They'll be responsible, independent, morally sound, and be able to build good relationships. All the things we want for our kids!

I'm sure you've realized by now that this balanced parenting style is my natural style of parenting. Of course, I'm joking. By nature, I tend to be overprotective and permissive. If I'm not careful, my three girls can wrap me around their little fingers. No one, by nature, has the balanced parenting style. All of us need to move away from our dysfunctional parenting styles and toward the balanced style.

The Road Ahead

I've only sketched the framework of the balanced parenting style in this chapter. In the chapters to follow I'll fill in the details and teach you the nuts and bolts of how to parent this way.

Identifying and adjusting your parenting style is important, but it isn't enough. It is only the first step on the road to becoming a balanced parent. Let's take a look now at the next step: working on four key relationships.

It Takes a Team

Your little pests—I mean, your precious children—are finally asleep. You and your partner have dropped into bed like two limp sacks of potatoes. You are sleeping the sleep of the truly exhausted. You are suddenly awakened by a cry in the night. You think to yourself: *Oh, no. Not again! Doesn't that kid ever sleep? I've got to have my rest tonight!*

You glance at the clock radio and inwardly cringe as your eyes make out the glowing numbers: 2:13 A.M. You hold perfectly still, hoping and praying that your oversensitive, selfish, whining child will be quiet and go back to sleep. Fat chance. Who are you kidding? When has that kid ever stopped a crying fit without help from a parent?

As the cries continue and increase in volume, you continue to hold perfectly still as you automatically shift to Plan B. You know what Plan B is, don't you? Now, you hope and pray that you can outlast your partner and she will have to get up and service the child. It's a difficult game of cat and mouse, demanding nerve, courage, and a great deal of pettiness—all of which you possess. The rules of the game are simple: Whoever moves first, loses.

Of course, history has taught you that either way you lose. If you get up, your sleep is ruined and you'll get very little thanks from your partner. If you outlast your spouse, your victory is hollow and short-lived. Your name is mud and you'll get a cold, critical reception in the morning from your loving spouse.

Our children present us with many challenges as they grow up. Some are minor, like a crying child in the middle of the night. Some are major and will cause you great worry, stress, and pain. You cannot afford to take the risk of facing these challenges alone. On your own, you will fail. It takes a team to raise a great kid (not a village).

Relationship with Spouse: A United Front

If you are married, your spouse is the most important member of your parenting team. You don't have to be married to be a good parent. But if you are married, it's important to build a solid, healthy marriage. If the two of you are unable to present a united front in dealing with your children, you're in trouble. In fact, it's a lost cause. Your children will defeat you.

Remember what I told you before: You are in a war with society for the hearts and minds of your children. You are also in a war with your own children! Kids are, by nature, selfish. They want what they want when they want it. If your kids are like mine, they're always scheming to get their way. If there is any daylight between a mom and a dad, kids will immediately jump into the opening and use it. They will seek to exploit the slightest difference between parents and turn it to their advantage. The strategy of divide and conquer didn't start with military generals. Hardly! Kids have been using this technique on their parents since the beginning of time.

God's Plan A is for a dad and a mom to be a real team in dealing with their kids. When you and your partner communicate and compromise in making parenting decisions, your kids don't have a chance. Sandy and I often disagree on how to handle situations with our four kids. We are two very different persons: two different sexes, two different personalities, two different family backgrounds, and two different parenting styles.

When a situation comes up with one of the kids, we talk about it privately. We pray about it together. We share our individual views on the issue and hash out our differences. We agree on a decision. Sometimes, Sandy has the best idea and we do it her way. Sometimes I have the best idea and we do it my way. Sometimes, we combine our two approaches and create a compromise position. When we present our decision to the child, we are in 100 percent agreement. The kid will desperately look for even the slightest shred of conflict or disagreement between us. If we've done our job, she will be disappointed to see an unbroken wall of parental solidarity.

When you build and maintain a great marriage, you're doing more than just improving your parenting. You are also modeling an intimate relationship between a man and a woman. Your kids will have many questions about opposite sex relationships. How do you meet the needs of a woman? How do you meet the needs of a man? How do you work through conflict? How do you create intimacy? Do you know where they'll get all their answers? From your relationship. Your sons' and daughters' relationships with the opposite sex are going to be just like your marriage relationship.

It's your choice. You can model a vibrant marriage. A marriage with mutual love and respect, open communication, and romance. Or you can model a poor marriage. A marriage with little time together, two separate lives, and no real emotional connection. It's really up to you. And please don't think for a minute your kids aren't aware of the quality of your marriage. Couples actually tell me, with straight faces: "Thank goodness our kids don't realize how unhappy we are." I say: "Dream on!

Are you serious? Your kids live with you. They have front-row seats! They miss nothing. They know just how good or bad your marriage is, and why."

There is no worse time to have a poor marriage than when you have kids in the house. Of course, there's no good time. But this is a particularly bad time. If your marriage is poor, you are setting your kids up to fail in their marriages. You are reproducing other poor marriages. Don't do that! Marriage was designed by God to be great. With God's help and hard work you can develop a great marriage. No matter how bad things are now, they can get better. If you need help, get it. See your pastor or a Christian therapist. Do it this week. If your partner refuses to go, then you go alone.

Single Parenting 101

Speaking of alone, I have a few things to say to you single parents. The bad news is, you are at a disadvantage and your job as a parent is much harder. You already know that. The entire load of parenting rests upon your shoulders. The good news is, you can do the job and do it well. Your kids can grow up as happy, healthy, and well-adjusted as kids from any family. Here are three ideas to make your job easier.

First, make sure that you and your kids have completely worked through the divorce, separation, or death of your spouse. A major loss like this has to be grieved. Feelings of anger, hurt, and guilt need to be expressed repeatedly over a period of months. For a family that works at it, it typically takes eighteen months to two years to adequately recover from the breakup of a family unit. Many kids I've seen in therapy have been stuck in the grieving process. They need to face the pain of loss and work through their feelings. Kids who are stuck in grieving get depressed. Their grades go down. They withdraw from friends and activities. They act out. Single parents, you don't need this. Losing your partner and adjusting to life and parenthood alone is enough. You don't want your kids to be damaged.

The key to healing is for you, the parent, to bring up the loss and express your feelings. Do this regularly, and do it in front of your kids. Stuffing your pain and being strong for your kids is a mistake. Without getting into the gory details, tell your kids why the marriage ended. Admit your own mistakes. Be honest and share your anger, deep hurt, and fear of going on alone. This will help you heal, motivate your kids to share their own pain, and bond you together as a family.

Second, do your best in your relationship with your ex-spouse. Easier said than done, I know. You can't control what your ex says and does. But you can control what you say and do, especially in front of your kids. You need to release all your anger and bitterness and hurt, forgive your ex, and move on. True forgiveness happens over time and requires continued expression of feelings. Express and release your feelings, as they come up, with your kids and with a close friend. You need to keep cleaning your system, continuing to forgive, and going forward with your life.

Don't keep fighting the same old battles with your ex! Sandy and I know couples who continue to rip and tear at each other well after their divorces. It's as though they never divorced. The same old unresolved issues come up again and again. They use their kids as pawns in an ongoing attempt to punish each other. It's wrong. It's pathetic. And it hurts the kids terribly. Divorce is bad enough. Don't keep on criticizing, sniping, and one-upping your ex. Grow up and act like an adult. You don't have to be best friends. Just try to be cordial and civil.

Third, make sure your relationships with the opposite sex are healthy. When you're dating someone, your children are watching and learning how to act in male-female relationships. You have a unique opportunity to teach dating principles. Don't blow it.

I once saw a single mom, her boyfriend, and the mom's teenage daughter in a therapy session. The mom, who was a Christian, had recently been caught by the daughter having sex with the boyfriend. She and the man wanted me to tell the daughter that their sex was okay. That everybody did it and it wasn't such a big deal. The daughter was horrified and demanded they stop having sex. I said: "When the kid's right, she's right. God says premarital sex is wrong. Confess your sin, apologize to your daughter, and stop it."

This couple was furious with me. They couldn't believe I was siding with their daughter. I wasn't siding with their daughter. I was siding with God. I told them: "Very soon now this young lady will be dating. What right will you have to tell her not to engage in sex? Unless you stop your sex immediately, your credibility will be zero." They weren't happy, but I think that got their attention.

Relationship with a Support System:
Don't Climb the Mountain Alone

Quick—name one person who has climbed Mount Everest alone. Go ahead. Can't do it, can you? That's because no one has ever done it. And no one ever will. It's just too hard to do on your own. The bitter, vicious cold. The sheer cliffs. The constant danger of avalanches. The dramatic, rapid changes in conditions. The jagged rocks. The massive ice sheets. The seemingly endless distance to the peak. If you want to make it to the top, you get help. When mountain climbers climb Mount Everest, they always go as a team.

Raising a child without support is like trying to climb Mount Everest alone. Actually, it's worse than that. Scaling Everest is a piece of cake compared to parenting. Don't try to do it by yourself. Even if you have a good, united relationship with your spouse, that's not enough. To be an effective parent, you need at least one close friend or couple outside the home for support. For practical advice. For brainstorming when you come up against a problem you can't figure out. For prayer.

Look, we all have parenting problems. Don't keep yours a secret! Do what Sandy and I have done. We have gathered around us a select group of family and friends who make up our parenting support team. We can discuss any personal or parenting problem with these loved ones. Our team includes three couples, a single parent, and both sets of grandparents.

The Bible says, in Ecclesiastes 4:12: "Though one may be overpowered, two can defend themselves. A cord of three strands is not quickly broken." Sandy and I have found this verse to be true. The members of our parenting team pray for our kids regularly. They give much-needed support and guidance. They love our kids and have good relationships with them. We could not do our job as parents without our team. We wouldn't even dare try.

Relationship with Self: Look in the Mirror

To a great degree, the quality of your personal life equals the quality of your parenting. You can't be any better as a parent than you are as a person. God gives us children, at least in part, to force us to face our weaknesses again. Our kids have the same personal problems we do. It's part genetics and part modeling. As my mother likes to say: "The acorn doesn't fall very far from the tree."

I have a confession to make. I have a smart mouth. It's a problem I've had ever since I was a kid. I'm the kind of guy who likes to joke around and tease. Most of the time, it's just innocent fun and people enjoy my kidding. But sometimes, I go a little too far with my mouth. My comments can be sharp, sarcastic, or inappropriate. Words just seem to come out, and afterward I wish I could take them back.

Guess who has two kids with smart mouths? I guess it's sweet justice. It's terrible to watch yourself grow up. My Emily, who's thirteen now, has a tendency to pop off just like dear old Dad. It's amazing how annoying it is to me to hear Emily doing her smart-mouth routine. When I call her on it, she shouts back: "You're one to talk, Dad. Where do you think I learned it? You do it all the time." What can I say?

It is my four-year-old son, William, however, who has taken the smart mouth to a whole new level. The kid definitely has the gift. A real chip off the old block. Let me give you a few recent examples. William, Emily, and Sandy were in the living room. Emily said something William didn't like, so he said to her in a loud, mean voice, "Shut your mouth!" Sandy said, "William! You can't talk that way. You have to say that in a much nicer way." William immediately turned to Emily, put his little hand on her knee, and said in a very sweet, kind, and soft voice: "Emily, shut your mouth." I don't think he got the point.

I found that episode funny because Emily was William's target. Several days later, I felt the sting of little Mister Clarke's smart mouth. The six of us were eating at one of our favorite restaurants. We were surrounded by people and having a great time pigging out on barbecue. William started to squirm and fidget. I said: "William, do you need to go to the bathroom? You already wet your briefs once today." William, not missing a beat, responded in a loud voice: "Dad, you wet your briefs sometimes, too!" I couldn't believe it. I said: "I do not! That's a lie!" From the looks I got from the people sitting around us, I think they wondered about me and my briefs.

What can you do about these weaknesses you and your children share? One thing you can do is work hard on your personal weaknesses. This is good for you. You'll be happier and healthier. It's also good for your kids. You can model for your kids how to work on their weaknesses. You never take a person farther than you've gone—spiritually or emotionally. Since your children have some of your personal problems, working on yours will help them work on theirs. If I really want Emily and William to improve in the smart-mouth area, I need to improve my smart mouth.

Another helpful action is to be honest with your children about your personal weaknesses. Let them know your weaknesses and allow them to see you working on them. How will your children learn to fix their personal problems unless you show them how? They won't. Far from frightening your children or causing insecurity, this kind of honesty will create a bond. I'm not suggesting you share intimate details of your personal, private struggles. You reserve this confidential information for a select few adults: spouse, best friend, pastor, therapist, accountability partner. But it's okay to give your kids a window in on some of the main weaknesses in your life. You don't have to share in detail. Just give them the basic sketch and update them on your progress.

When I was growing up, my dad was open with me (and my brother Mark) about his self-esteem problem. I remember being blown away by this revelation, because I never would have guessed he had a problem liking himself. My dad was (and is) a very bright, godly, and successful man. Dad's openness in this very personal area impressed me. I felt like I could relate to him better. I didn't feel like he was perfect or above me, but that he was struggling, too. Here was a man in the real world, grappling with real problems. I felt closer to my dad. And his example has helped me deal more effectively with my own self-esteem issues.

Relationship with God: The Power Source

Without question, your relationship with God is the most important relationship in your life. I'm talking about your personal relationship with God. How will a healthy relationship with God help you be an effective parent? In two critical ways.

First, God provides you with the power to be a good parent. God is the power source of all good and wise parenting. Without God's help, you can't adjust your parenting style. Without God's help, you won't have the patience, the insight, and the endurance it takes to raise healthy kids. Parenting is a supernatural job. Don't try it without God! Read what Philippians 4:13 has to say:

I can do everything through him who gives me strength.

The "Him" is Jesus Christ. And the "everything" includes parenting. I want God and Jesus Christ on my side. I want their help on a daily basis with my kids. Don't you?

Second, when you have a close relationship with God through Jesus Christ, you will model a godly, moral lifestyle. Modeling is the most effective way to teach and influence others. What you say is not nearly as important as what you do. Jesus Christ taught by modeling and it worked! The disciples lived with Christ. They worked with Him. They ate with Him. And they were never the same. They learned how to be godly men by watching Jesus.

We have the same opportunity with our kids! We have to show our kids how to live in our rotten, morally bankrupt culture. Every day, your child will compare your life with the world. He'll look at your life: a life with God, based on the Bible, with morals and values—and, it is hoped, he'll find them too. He'll look at the world: a life without God, with no values, no right and wrong, with the only guide what feels good. My fellow parents, your kid had better see a dramatic difference between you and the world! If your Christian life isn't too good, what makes you think your child will want it? He won't! With God's help, show him that the Christian life works and is the best choice.

Let me ask you a question: How are you doing in your personal relationship with God? Honestly. If you don't have a personal relationship with God, you can begin that relationship today. Right now, if you want. You can have a relationship with God only through His Son, Jesus Christ (John 14:6; Acts 4:12). Admit to God that you are a sinner, and that on your own you can never reach Him. Believe that Jesus Christ, God's only Son, died on a cross for all your sins. Believe that Jesus literally rose from the dead three days after His crucifixion. Tell God you believe what Jesus did for you, and from that instant you are a Christian. You have the most precious gift in the universe: a relationship with God.

If you already are a Christian, how is your relationship with God? I don't want to hear: "Oh, okay." Okay's not good enough. Okay isn't enough to really connect you with God's power. Okay isn't enough to convince your kids the Christian life is worthwhile. You need to work on your relationship with God. Spend private time with God each day—praying, reading the Bible, and just being with Him.

When you know God and are growing in that relationship, you have the power to live life. You have the power to build good relationships. And you have the power to be a good and effective parent.

NINE

Give the Gift of Self-Esteem

The High Cost of Kids

Allll good parents give their children gifts. Toys. Clothes. Swing sets. Video games. Computers. Summer camps. Trips to amusement parks. Cars. Insurance. College education. Am I depressing you? The list is endless. Once a year, the newspapers print the astronomical figure it will cost you to raise a child from birth through college. Now, before I state the current figure, let me recommend a few precautionary measures.

If you don't feel emotionally ready to read the figure, just skip down several paragraphs. Or get someone you love right now and have that person sit with you as you read it. And make sure all sharp objects are out of your reach. I'm perfectly serious. I've had parents run screaming from the room after hearing it in one of my parenting workshops. These poor souls just completely broke down, sobbing uncontrollably and curling up in the fetal position. It was embarrassing. Understandable, but embarrassing.

Well, for those of you brave enough to face the truth, here it is. The current amount of money it takes to raise one child through college is: $400,000. That's for one child! That's assuming your child attends a state college or university. That's a lot of money. We parents give and give and give, and give some more to our children.

The Number Two Priority

Many parents, however, fail to give one critically important gift to their children. If you fail to give this gift, two things happen, both bad. First, your children will be vulnerable and unprotected as they grow up. They will be susceptible to the negative influences of our culture. And we have plenty of negative influences, don't we? Second, as adults, your children will be limited in many ways. The lack of this gift affects your children well into adulthood.

If you succeed in giving this gift, two things happen, both good. First, your children will be protected as they grow up. They will have a fighting chance against our culture's attacks. I should say, Satan's attacks, because he's in charge of our culture (1 John 5:19). You can't change Satan or the culture, but you can give something to your kids to help them in the fight. Second, you will provide your kids with a healthy foundation for the rest of their lives.

The gift I'm talking about is healthy self-esteem. One of your most important jobs as a parent is to be actively building the self-esteem of your children. This is second only to bringing your children to Christ and nurturing them spiritually. The critical impact of self-esteem on your children's lives cannot be overstated. Simply put, the level of your children's self-esteem will largely determine the level of their success in every major area of life. With this gift of solid self-esteem, you give your child the best opportunity to be psychologically healthy, do well in a career, have quality relationships, and develop a deep faith in God.

The Bad Rap on Self-Esteem

Self-esteem has gotten a bad rap lately, especially in some Christian circles. In my opinion, this bad rap is a bum rap. Christian pastors, theologians, and others who rail against self-esteem do not understand the true meaning of self-esteem. They say self-esteem is a worldly, egocentric, ungodly focus on self. They say self-esteem is placing yourself in the driver's seat of life and pushing God out of the car. They say self-esteem turns you into a completely selfish person who ignores the needs of others. They say self-esteem is nothing less than the tool of the devil.

You know something? These Christian leaders are right, because there is a worldly, ungodly type of self-esteem. No question about it. I strongly oppose this kind of secular self-esteem. But these Christian leaders are dead wrong, too, because there is a Christ-centered, biblical type of self-esteem. The kind of self-esteem I'm talking about in this book is the self-esteem God talks about in the Bible. God wants us to love ourselves and accept His view of us in Christ. When we believe we can do all things through Him, we can genuinely love others and serve them.

Let's look at the Bible. Love of self and love of others are tied together by God:

In this same way,
husbands ought to love their wives as their own bodies.
He who loves his wife loves himself.
After all, no one ever hated his own body,
but he feeds and cares for it,
just as Christ does the church.
EPHESIANS 5:28–29

> *Jesus replied, " 'Love the Lord your God with*
> *all your heart and with all your soul*
> *and with all your mind.'*
> *This is the first and greatest commandment.*
> *And the second is like it:*
> *'Love your neighbor as yourself.' "*
> MATTHEW 22:37–39

I believe God is saying that you cannot love others without loving yourself. In fact, you need to love others the way you love yourself. You see, you can only reach out and meet the needs of others when you have a confident, secure love of self. When you love self in a Christ-centered, healthy way, you get self out of the way. You can then spend your time and energy loving your neighbor.

It's All about Needs

You ask, "But what is this Christ-centered, healthy self-esteem, and how can I give it to my children?" Good question. Let me define self-esteem. This is perhaps the finest definition of self-esteem you will ever see. Of course, it's my own.

Healthy self-esteem is a realistic and positive view of self achieved when five needs are consistently met:

- Love
- Respect
- Competence
- Spirituality
- Independence

What I'm telling you is that if you meet these five needs in the lives of your children, they will develop healthy self-esteem. It will work even for those children born with a tendency to not like themselves. This need-driven approach will work no matter how old your kids are. It will work no matter what mistakes you've made as parents up to now. In other words, it's never too late to turn your children around and lead them into a healthy self-esteem.

Let's take a look at the great child-rearing advice given in Ephesians 6:4. In this verse, parents are instructed to "bring them up in the training and instruction of the Lord." A key part of the meaning of the phrase "bring them up" is to meet the needs of children. If you meet the needs of your children, you will obey God. And you will build into your children the self-esteem God wants them to have.

I need to warn you that this gift of self-esteem isn't cheap or easy to give. It's going to cost you in time, effort, and changes in your lifestyle. Self-esteem doesn't just happen. You, the parent, make it happen! So, it will cost you to give it. But believe me, it will cost you and your children far more if you fail to give it.

What you need is a strategy for meeting each one of the five needs. That's exactly what the next five chapters will give you. When you've read these chapters, you will know the practical steps necessary to give your children the great gift of self-esteem.

Love Me Tender

P acifier. It sounds so sweet. So soothing. So gentle. Such a helper and friend to a parent. Just pop a pacifier in and your child is happy, content, and. . .well. . .pacified. Yeah. Right. As a brand-new parent, I believed these shameless lies cranked out by the pacifier industry. I found out the hard way that the pacifier was no friend of mine. It made my life a living nightmare for two solid years. Since *60 Minutes* doesn't have the guts to expose the pacifier hoax, I'll do it myself.

Our first child (and very nearly our last), Emily, became extremely attached to the first pacifier we put into her mouth. It was like she bonded to that pacifier and not to us. We, her own, caring parents, couldn't comfort her when she was upset. We couldn't quiet her down. The only thing that worked was that pacifier. She had to have the pacifier to stop crying. She had to have that pacifier to take a nap. She had to have that pacifier to go to sleep at night. Every night, when it was bedtime, Emily would say, "Brush the teeth, and pacifier." It became a ritual set in stone.

She knew that pacifier intimately: every curve, every stain, every tooth mark. It was the only pacifier she'd take into her screaming, whining, pouting little mouth. We bought three others just like it, but she refused to accept them. She'd immediately spit the imposter out of her mouth, throw it to the floor, and yell, "That's not my pacifier!" You know what happened next, don't you?

We'd have to turn the house upside down looking for that no-good, stupid, time-wasting, blood-sucking, $1.99 pacifier! Oh, I can remember as though it were yesterday those mad, desperate searches. Emily would throw that pacifier down in the strangest places and, of course, she'd never know where it was. That wasn't her problem.

The middle of the night searches were the worst. Emily would wake up, realize the pacifier was not in her mouth, and instantly scream for help. When it was my turn, I'd stumble into her room and fumble around looking for it: in the bed sheets and blankets, underneath the bed, on the floor, wedged between the wall and crib, caught in the bars of the crib. . . That pacifier wound up in some bizarre, incredibly hard-to-find places. One night, I searched for twenty minutes, with no success. I put my hand on Emily's heaving little stomach and felt the pacifier! It had fallen down her pajama top and was resting against her belly button! I think she knew it was there the whole time.

Sandy and I were slaves to that pacifier. It ran our miserable lives. I hated that pacifier, but I was powerless against it. But then one beautiful day, the sun broke through and light shone into my dark world of torment. It was the day we broke Emily's pacifier habit. I will never forget that day. She called for her pacifier at bedtime, but she didn't get it. She screamed and yelled and sobbed for one solid hour. Sandy was upset and felt sorry for Emily. I pretended to be sympathetic, but I was a happy man. I was finally being released from prison.

Sandy wanted to comfort Emily. It looked like she was considering giving the pacifier back to Emily! It was at that moment that I really and truly became a man. The leader of my home. Desperate times demand desperate measures. Summoning my courage, I said, "It's me or the pacifier!" I didn't like the way Sandy paused. Fortunately, she made the right choice.

The next day, I took the pacifier outside and placed it on the cold, hard concrete driveway. I said to it, "It's over, pacifier! You've had a nice run, but it's over. Now, you pay for your crimes." I took my trusty hammer and crushed the pacifier into little pieces. Then I threw my head back and, in a loud voice, said, "Free at last! Free at last! I'm finally free at last!"

Of course, I wasn't free for long. We were through with pacifiers, but the three kids who followed simply latched on to other inanimate objects. Leeann, Nancy, and William gave the term "security blanket" a whole new meaning. Talk about having a blanket fetish! Leeann had two special blankets she called Pink and Green. Nancy had a moth-eaten, shot-full-of-holes, multicolored blanket I referred to as "the rag." William, at four, has two dingy, stained, yellow blankets he has to have in the car and at bedtime.

And don't even get me started on stuffed animals. Each of my kids has about thirty precious animal friends. I have spent the best years of my life searching for blankets and stuffed animals. I can recall many times when we turned the car around to go back to a friend's home to retrieve a stuffed animal. I wanted to run the animal over with my car, but I didn't do that. I'm a kind man. A caring man. And I can't stand screaming in the car. So I went back.

Why do small kids get so attached to pacifiers, blankets, stuffed animals, and other objects? It's because kids are sensitive, tenderhearted little creatures. It's not easy being small in a big world. Kids have insecurities and fears. These special objects help children cope with the scary parts of life. They offer a certain measure of comfort and security. "It's not just me in this big, dark room. It's me and my pacifier." Or, "Me and Teddy Bear." So, it's perfectly okay to give your kids these objects. Go ahead and search for them when they get lost.

But, parents, you need to realize that these objects provide only a temporary and superficial solution to your children's fears of being alone and vulnerable. Over the long term, real security and comfort come only when you meet the deepest need of your children. That need is love.

Love Is Everything

Love is the greatest human need. It is impossible to over-emphasize the importance of love in the life of children. Quite literally, love is the very breath of life for every human being. To grow and develop normally, love is required. Chapter 13 of Paul's First Epistle to the Corinthians makes it clear that, without love, we have nothing and we are nothing. The final verse in Paul's great chapter on love says it all:

And now these three remain: faith, hope and love.
But the greatest of these is love.
1 CORINTHIANS 13:13

Your child has a desperate need to be loved by you. I've talked with a lot of kids who are not really sure their parents love them. I ask these kids, "Do your parents love you?" Very often, they pause. Not a good sign. Then, all too often, they reply, "Well, I guess so." My friends, that's not good enough. What would your kid tell me?

Your job as a parent is to make your love for your child crystal clear. This will give her a foundation to stand on when everything else in her world is chaotic. Growing up is tough and getting tougher all the time. Knowing she is loved, and feeling that love, gives her the confidence to face the world and win.

Love is action. Doing loving things is what communicates love. Parents tell me all the time: "I love my kids. I really do. I'm sure they know it." My response is, "How? How do they know it?" You'd better make good and sure they know it. Love not communicated is worthless. It's nothing. It's not love at all. Here are some actions that any parent, single or married, can do to communicate love to a child.

The Every-Days

For the past ten years, Sandy and I have been doing four things every day to communicate love to our children. We have found that when each child receives these four things, a healthy dose of love is administered. It's like getting a booster shot every day. This system has worked for us, and it will work for you.

First, we say, "I love you" to each kid. These are the most beautiful words in any language. They are 100 percent positive words. They are healing words. We use the child's name to make it personal. "I love you, Emily." "I love you, Leeann." "I love you, Nancy." "I love you, William." And we don't say the words in a flippant, breezy way. We use a soft, meaningful tone to make sure the message gets across. We do this at least once a day, and often two or three times.

I can't tell you how many times I've heard these words in

my therapy office from adult clients: "Dave, my dad—or mom—never said to me, 'I love you.' " These clients are usually sobbing when they tell me this. They want desperately to hear these words, but many never will. I've heard many stories of clients waiting in vain by the deathbed of a parent, hoping to hear, "I love you." It's heartbreaking. It's not right! If you can't say these words, take speech lessons. Get therapy. Your children's self-esteem is at stake.

The second daily action Sandy and I practice is physical touch. Every one of our kids gets touched in an affectionate, caring way every day. A hug. A kiss. A rub of the neck. A squeeze of the shoulder. What's the largest organ in the human body? It's the skin! God gave us so much skin because He wants it to be touched. Touch feels warm. It feels caring. It feels like love.

During World War II, England was bombed mercilessly by the Nazis. Because so many parents were killed in the bombing raids, the government was forced to establish a network of orphanages in rural areas. Some years ago, several researchers studied one particular English orphanage. Using records kept by the orphanage workers, they followed one group of children from the time they arrived at the orphanage as infants to their adulthood. One aspect of the study was the impact of touch on the lives of these orphans. Their results are fascinating and revealing.

The researchers found that, in this orphanage, for reasons unknown, one group of babies was touched, and one group of babies was not touched. The babies not touched by the workers developed many problems. A high percentage of these unfortunate kids died in the orphanage. They never made it out of infancy. "Failed to thrive" was the depressing phrase written in their charts. Those untouched babies who did survive had all kinds of problems as adults: physical disabilities, emotional problems, and involvement in crime. Very few of these kids became healthy, productive members of English society.

The babies who were touched and physically nurtured by the orphanage employees fared dramatically better. Most of these children survived infancy and developed into stable, productive citizens. The vast majority were physically and emotionally healthy. At least as healthy as you can be when you grow up in an orphanage.

It doesn't take a genius to figure out the lesson of this story. You'd better lovingly touch your kids, and you'd better touch them every day. Some of you are thinking, *But Dave, I'm just not an affectionate person. I'm not the touchy, huggy type.* My response is simple: "Get over it!" The stakes are too high to use this cop-out. Learning to touch your kids may be very awkward at first. You'll feel like Frankenstein stumping toward your kids—stiff, unnatural, and uncoordinated. Just keep practicing. You'll get it. And your kids will get the physical expression of love they desperately need.

This touching stuff is easier with young children. Most of the time they run to you and begin touching. Young kids love to give and receive touch. If you have a teenager, you've got to be clever. Take off your shoes and sneak up behind your teen and squeeze his shoulder. He'll say, "Oh, man, cut it out!" But, deep down, he'll like it. Teenagers need touch as much, if not more, than younger kids.

The third everyday action is eating one meal together. What is it about food? There's something about sharing a meal that brings us closer. Plus, it's a family time. A time when everybody is together and real connections can be made. In our home, as in most homes, this daily meal is breakfast or dinner. Some days we eat both meals together. But those days are rare. We've found that even five or ten minutes at breakfast, when we're all together, communicates love. Even though the kids are half-asleep with their heads hanging over their cereal bowls, it still works. There's a feeling of family as we sit in a circle around the table. There's a feeling of love.

Fourth, Sandy and I share one personal item each day. By personal I mean a feeling, a need, a painful experience, a victory, or a spiritual insight. When we share something personal, it means, "We love you." We open up and show our kids a piece of who we are inside. This kind of vulnerability creates a love connection between parents and children. Also, it models sharing. When Mom and Dad share, it's more likely the kids will open up and share. It sends the message: "In this family, we openly share our feelings, and talk honestly and personally."

I'm sure those of you reading this are bright persons. I'll bet you've figured out by now that you can do all four "every-days" at the same time. (I'm trying to help you not only with parenting, but also with time management.) Picture this scene. It's evening and everyone is sitting around the dinner table. You make your way around the table, touching each child and saying, "I love you." Two every-days down. You're already having a meal together, so that's three. If you sit down and share something personal—boom! You've taken care of all four every-days. Every single kid at that table gets a shot of love, right in the kisser.

You Gotta Spend Time

For children of all ages, love is measured in time. Without time, there is no love. There couldn't be. Without time together, there is no personal relationship. When the right amount of time is provided, love is clearly and powerfully communicated. You ask, "How much time, and what kind of time?" Here are some ideas.

Establish a once-a-week family meeting. With the rapid pace of life and all the different schedules of the family members, this won't be easy. Do it anyway, because it's important. Attendance is mandatory. This is a twenty- to thirty-minute meeting. No distractions allowed. Let the phone ring. Do not answer the door. Turn off the television, the computer, radio, CD player, etc. The purpose of the meeting is to check in and see how everybody is doing, deal with any problems in or outside the family, and have fun together.

Each family member, beginning with the parents, shares what's going on in his or her personal life. Good things. Difficult things. Problems. Spiritual things. If a member is hurting or struggling, the family comes together to help that person. Support, advice, and prayer are given. As families, I believe we are to follow Paul's exhortation in Romans 12:15: "Rejoice with those who rejoice; mourn with those who mourn." We can't do this unless we spend time as a family and know what's happening in the life of each member.

The family meeting is supposed to include fun, too. When I was a kid, we'd often spend the last part of a family meeting playing a zany game called Mad Libs. This game consisted of written stories that were incomplete. With no idea of what the story was about, family members supplied parts of speech— nouns, adverbs, verbs, to fill in the blanks and complete the stories. The results were hilarious. These days, the six of us sometimes play Mad Libs during the fun part of our family meetings. We also play board games, charades, or cards. I am the master of Crazy Eights.

Family times are important, but they're not enough. When you have all the kids together, it's usually total chaos. The squabbling, the fighting, and the petty bickering often limit the quality of the time together. "She touched me!" "He made a bad smell!" "She said a bad word." And on and on.

One-on-one, you can really connect and build the relationships. Therefore, I also strongly recommend that you offer several hours of individual time to each child once every two or three weeks. I say *offer* because teenagers won't always take you up on invitations. After a certain age, being seen with Mom or Dad is the absolute kiss of social death. You suddenly become a leper—someone to be tolerated, pitied, and avoided at all costs. Teens will take your money, but your presence is not welcomed. However, if you're willing to do an activity your teenagers really enjoy, you just might entice the kids to spend time with you.

In this individual time, do what the kid wants to do. Forcing a kid to tag along on your activity of choice does not communicate love. It communicates selfishness. It doesn't matter if you don't like your kid's chosen activity. It's even better if you don't like it, because then your kid really knows you love him. For years, my dad played golf with me because I loved the game. My dad hated golf, and he wasn't very good at it. As I watched my dad struggle around the golf course, hitting one horrendous shot after another, I knew two things were true: First, my dad was a terrible golfer. Second, my dad loved me.

I'm talking about one-on-one time between fathers and sons, mothers and daughters, fathers and daughters, and mothers and sons. Don't fall into the common trap of just investing time with your same-sex kids. No, no, no! It's easier and more natural for moms to focus on daughters and dads to focus on sons. But this robs your opposite-sex kids of the chance to get to know you and feel loved by you.

Now that my three girls are older and finally out of the Barbie stage—thank God—I take them on lunch dates. (I told you about my experience with Barbies in my book *Men Are Clams, Women Are Crowbars.*) This is what they want to do, so I do it. It gives them the opportunity to do what they enjoy most: talk. The girls want it to be a real date, so here's what I have to do. With my date watching from the window, I go outside the house and get in my car. I get out of my car and walk to my front door and ring the doorbell. My date says in a sweet voice, "Who is it?" I think to myself, *What do you mean, who is it? You just saw me walk up to the door.* Of course, I don't say that. I say, "It's Daddy, your date." I go to the restaurant my date selects. I hold the car door open for her. I hold her hand as we walk. I get her chair at the restaurant. I listen to her talk. . . and talk, and talk, and talk. And I have a wonderful time. And so does she.

I play sports with my four-year-old, William. He is a sports fanatic: baseball, football, basketball, you name it. But his favorite sport (and mine, coincidentally) is golf. We putt golf balls inside the house on the carpet. We watch golf on television. We hit golf balls in the front yard and down the street. Lately, we play Putt-Putt golf every Wednesday morning (my morning off). We take our own putters because we're serious golfers. I'm telling you, the kid is good. He wins half the Putt-Putt rounds we play. Just this last week, he made three holes-in-one in a row and beat me by three shots. It's pretty humiliating to lose to a four year old! Actually, I don't care. William and I are together. That's all that counts.

An Open-Door Policy

One more way you communicate love is by telling your kids that they are free to come to you with any topic, at any time. Nothing is off-limits! When your kids are in trouble, tempted, or have a question about life, you want them to come to you. Don't you? In so many homes, there are issues that can't be discussed: sex, discrimination, abortion, the occult, rock music, moral issues, spiritual questions, getting along with others and relationships. . . .

Parents, listen to me. Being a kid these days is hard. Incredibly hard. The culture pounds away at your child every hour of every day. Thousands of messages from the pit of hell bombard him: "If it feels good, do it." "Premarital sex is great fun and everybody's doing it." "Homosexuality is a completely normal, healthy lifestyle." "Go ahead and cheat if you can get away with it." "Morality is whatever you choose to believe." "You have unlimited, divine power inside." "There is no God." And these messages are wrapped in beautiful, seductive packages.

It's critical that you encourage your child to talk to you about the culture's misinformation. If your kid doesn't talk to you, you'll lose her. Culture and Satan will win the war. But if you can open an honest, two-way dialogue with your child, you can correct culture's misconceptions and outright lies. You can beat culture and Satan at their deadly game. You, and your child, will take some hits. But in the end, with communication lines open and in steady use, you'll win the war.

ELEVEN

I Don't Get No Respect!

"Where's Your Spaceship, Sweetheart?"

The fourteen-year-old person came in the door of my office, just ahead of her parents. I say "person" because, at first glance, I couldn't tell what sex I had on my hands. My second look confirmed that she was, indeed, a female. The parents shuffled in, looking like refugees from a lost war. They looked uneasy, as though they were both about to throw up. I was soon to understand the reason for their chronic feeling of nausea.

As the family of three settled into their chairs, I took a good, long look at the girl. What a sight! She had spiked hair with orange and blue clumps shooting up at random angles. Pieces of string and jewelry were tied around some of the hair clumps. She wore makeup that would have made Tammy Faye Bakker jealous. It was bright white and at least a foot thick. Her earrings were as big as wind chimes. Of course, she didn't just have earrings in her ears. It looked as if every available spot on her body had been pierced and a ring inserted—a ring through her eyebrow, a ring through her nose, a ring through her tongue, and a ring through her navel. She was apparently proud of her navel ornament because it was on display. She wore wild, striped clothes that looked like they'd been salvaged from the site of a '70s disco bombing. The girl looked like an alien, pure and simple.

As a shrewd and tactful therapist, I knew it was important to gain this girl's trust and build rapport as quickly as possible. So, I said to her, "Where's your spaceship, sweetheart?" I thought her parents were going to have a conniption right there in my office. The kid actually got a kick out of my question. After my rather ragged beginning, I took a history and found out what I already knew: This girl had no respect. No respect for herself. No respect for her parents. No respect for anyone. Not even her weird friends.

Her parents were permissive, and they were paying a dear price for that parenting style. This girl had zero self-esteem, because without respect, self-esteem dies. Her outrageous appearance and contempt for her parents masked a deep sense of personal shame and self-loathing. The main presenting problem was that she had decided to stop attending school. She was, in fact, refusing to do anything her parents wanted her to do.

The key to the case was building respect. As the parents got tough and laid down clear limits and consequences, the girl began to respect them. As communication improved in the family, she began to earn her parents' respect. Finally, she began to respect herself. Her clothing even improved. She wasn't wearing dresses, but at least she didn't look like a character from *The Munsters.*

This is, of course, an extreme example of what can happen when a child has no respect. But, believe me, damage to self-esteem is always done when respect is absent. Let's look at some practical ways to meet the need for respect in your child's life.

Know Your Limits

I'll begin with a description of respect. Respect is establishing clear boundaries between you and others. A person with respect knows the limits between himself and others. He doesn't cross the line to mistreat others, and doesn't allow others to mistreat him without responding. Respect is essential to both healthy self-esteem and good relationships with others. If a child has respect, he will treat himself and others with dignity, concern, and fairness. He will not destroy himself or let others destroy him.

You build respect into your children with limits—and there are two kinds of limits. There are the limits you place on your children. You set clear boundaries in your home and enforce them consistently. You draw up—with your spouse and support system—the rules of the house. You present these rules to your children and say, "Here are the boundaries of your life. We believe staying inside these boundaries is what the Lord wants. They will keep you safe and help you develop into healthy and godly persons. If you decide to cross a boundary, we will apply consequences." I go into detail on these kinds of limits in my chapters on discipline.

Limits of the second type are those you allow your children to place on you. Many parents aren't aware that limits go both ways. Respect your child's privacy. Knock before entering your child's room. This is common courtesy. I've had to learn this with my three daughters. I don't want to barge in when they're dressing and embarrass them and myself. They have to knock on my door, so it's only right that I knock on their doors. Don't misunderstand me. I'm the parent, and I own the house. So, I'm going to come into the room. They won't be allowed to keep me out. But I can grant them the respect of waiting a few minutes. "Are you ready to receive your honored visitor, my dear?"

Unless you have solid justification, don't read your kid's mail, E-mail, or diaries. Don't listen in on her telephone conversations. Don't search or tidy up her room. It's better for your health to stay out of her room, anyway. I've known parents who went into a kid's room without proper safety precautions and never made it out. They were overcome by the noxious fumes and hazardous wastes. Your kid survives in there because she has built up immunity to that poisonous environment. If you need to go into the room, send in a small rodent first (of course, there may already be some rodents in there). If it's still alive after ten minutes, you're probably okay to go in.

If you have a good reason, however, don't hesitate to violate every area of your child's privacy. If you suspect trouble, go through the kid's room with a fine-tooth comb. I've sent many parents home to turn a kid's room inside out. Read all the mail you can get your hands on. Eavesdrop on phone conversations. Talk to their friends, other parents, and school officials. Your kid will scream bloody murder and threaten never to forgive you. Fine. Forgiveness isn't the issue. Correcting a serious problem and saving your child is the issue.

Communication Is the Key

You meet the need for respect in your children with communication skills. Communicating effectively with other adults is difficult enough, especially if the relationship is a personal one: spouse, friend, or family member. Communicating effectively with children is incredibly difficult. They're immature, and they don't yet have the tools to communicate well. In short, kids don't know what they're doing in the area of communication. It's your job as the parent to teach them the basic skills of connecting in a conversation. When you teach these skills, you'll build more than just a good relationship. You'll build respect.

You need to learn to listen to your child. James 1:19 gives us a great communication principle: "Everyone should be quick to listen, slow to speak and slow to become angry." Many parents (including me) are slow to listen, quick to speak, and quick to get angry with their child. I'm working hard at listening, and I want you to work at it, too. So many conversations with a kid are lost in the first few sentences because the parent reacts, cuts in, and interrupts. My fellow parents, if you want your kid to listen to you, you've got to model by listening to him. If you want to keep a conversation alive, you've got to listen. The first thing, the very first thing, you do when your child speaks, is listen. Say nothing. Just listen with your big mouth closed.

After your child has gotten several paragraphs out and is warming up, you can move to the second thing: Reflect your child's emotions. Notice that you still have not said anything original in this conversation. And you won't for a while. By reflecting, you can communicate understanding of your child's emotions, whatever they are—anger, hurt, humiliation, frustration, fear, joy. . . Your child feels understood when you identify and give back her emotions. In other words, it's all about what your kid is saying and feeling in the first part of a conversation. "Is this what you are feeling about what you are saying, Susan?" You will have all kinds of thoughts and feelings of your own as your kid talks. Stuff these until it's your turn. If you jump in before you communicate understanding, you violate respect, and the conversation is over. You may be talking, but no one's going to be listening. Why should your kid listen to you? You weren't listening to her.

As in the case of limits, there is an exception to this. You don't bother reflecting when your kid is out of control: yelling, using profanity, or being verbally abusive. When Jimmy has lost it and is tearing into you verbally, you don't say, "Jimmy, what I hear you saying is you hate Mommy. You're very angry, and Mommy makes you sick." Of course not. Jimmy has violated respect for you, and you bring this particular conversation to a halt: "Young man, that's enough. When you can calm down, apologize, and can talk to me in a reasonable way, we will continue this conversation."

It's very tough to reflect with angry kids. They're emotionally intense. They fight dirty. They know your weaknesses and will deliberately say things to inflame you. Look, your kids really don't want to talk with you when they're upset, hurt, or angry. They're masters at getting you to react, and when you do, that ends the conversation. Fool them by listening and reflecting and maybe—just maybe—you'll get a real conversation.

Your daughter comes to you and says, "I failed my math test today." She could say this in a number of different ways. You listen, and reflect the proper emotion: "You're really angry about that," or, "You seem depressed, hurt, like you're ready to quit," or, "You seem happy and relaxed" (that would not be a good sign). You table your reaction and reflect in order to build understanding first. Later, you move to some solution and to your own feelings. Even if your child says something outrageous and obviously not true, reflect first. Your child is much more likely to talk and share and listen, if you are listening and reflecting.

Recently, I saw a couple who had two daughters, ages ten and six. They were having tremendous problems with the ten year old. They described her as difficult, mouthy, and selfish. I didn't mention this, but the mother was also difficult, mouthy, and selfish. Very often, the kid who drives us nuts is the kid who is most like us. This girl was sulking, whining, and disobedient. These parents couldn't seem to hold a decent conversation with their daughter. After just a few sentences, all three would be yelling and saying all kinds of nasty things they didn't really mean.

The problem was, the parents weren't listening and reflecting. In therapy, I forced them to be quiet and to listen to what the girl was saying. Frankly, the kid was difficult to listen to because she had an annoying, whining style of speech. But, as they listened, they realized what was really happening. Underneath the mouthy, disobedient exterior was a little girl who felt rejected. She told them she felt her younger sister was being praised more often and with more enthusiasm. She said they expected more from her because she was older and it was hard to please them. They realized she was right. Because she was the firstborn and a more difficult child, they were being too hard on her. When they acknowledged this to her, their daughter felt understood; they extended the conversation and found out her true feelings and were able to solve the problem. All because they listened and reflected. And because they had a great therapist. (Just kidding.)

When your child is talking, make sure there are no distractions or outside interference of any kind. Establish eye contact. Listen, and reflect, and build understanding. Then, only after you have done this, and it is your turn, teach your child to listen to you and to feed back what you are saying and feeling. That's good communication. That's one of the ways you build respect.

Speak Your Child's Language

Something I've learned in the past few years is that each of my four children has a natural, chosen style of communication. It's their own, unique language. It's how they express themselves. If I really want to connect with them, it makes no sense to use my style of communication. I need to use their styles of communication.

My Emily, thirteen, is a writer. She loves to express herself in writing, and she is good at it. She's always sending friends and family members notes and letters. When she really wants to get a point across, she writes. Guess what I need to do if I really want to get a point across to Emily? That's right. I sit down and write her a note. Since that's her language, it works like a charm. After she reads my note, she'll usually respond with a note. We usually end up talking about it, but the main avenue with Emily is the written word.

My Leeann, eleven, is a talker. She loves to talk and uses a lot of words to express herself. She is a highly verbal person and a very interesting conversationalist. She'll use great detail in describing situations, events, and concerns in her life. No detail is too small for Leeann. She tells long stories, often using word pictures to illustrate her point. When I want to reach Leeann in a conversation, I talk the way she talks. I try to use details, more words, and word pictures. I may describe a movie I've seen or use an elaborate analogy in order to make my point. Leeann appreciates this approach and my messages get across. Of course, I need to make sure I set aside a good twenty minutes because Leeann will respond to my detailed story with one of her own.

My Nancy, eight, is a smaller version of my mother. What

that means, communication-wise, is that Nancy wastes no words. She is straightforward, direct, and blunt. When Nancy has something to say, she says it. No frills. No details. No beating around the bush. So when I talk to Nancy, I cut to the chase. I say what I have to say straight out. She'd never tolerate a long, involved story. Life's too short for that. She just wants to get to the point.

My William, four, is a typical guy. Unlike the girls, I can't just sit down and talk with him. If I tried that, I'd lose him after five seconds. He's always moving, always doing something, and he talks and shares himself as he plays.

So how do I talk to William about things that really matter? I talk to him in short spurts as we play together. Sometimes I relate what I'm saying to the sport or activity in which we're engaged. "William, great shot! You didn't stop trying to hit the hole with your five iron even though your first ten shots missed. It's important to keep trying. Right?" William takes in my message because it's given as part of an activity. Find out your children's style of communication, and use it. If you use each child's preferred language, your messages will get across, and your kids will open up. It works!

Here are two more communication ideas that work. One, talk to your kids before they go to sleep. When it's the end of the day and they're finally winding down, you have a good opportunity to slip a message into their heads and maybe from there to their hearts. Their brain waves are different. Their defenses are down. They're more mellow. You can sit on the edge of the bed or lie down beside them and do some neat connecting. They may also tell you things that they wouldn't have earlier in the day. Two—and this goes with One—pray out loud at bedtime. A brief prayer saying some things you want them to hear is a great way to communicate. Don't lay it on too thick. Be subtle and tactful. Because it's directed to the Lord, not to them, they tend to be less defensive; they can take what you pray to heart.

Don't Break Your Kid

Never belittle your child's looks, abilities, habits, mannerisms, or performance. This is a serious breach of respect! Kids are fragile. They are extremely sensitive. You can literally break them with careless comments and sharp criticism. I've talked to many kids who have suffered deep, lasting wounds from a parent's mouth. They do not recover from verbal assaults easily. There is no place for sarcasm or put-downs. Even if they do it to you, make sure you don't retaliate.

"I'm Sorry"

Let's be honest. We all blow it occasionally. I sure do. Ever spanked the wrong kid? I have. I've come upon the scene of the crime and made a too hasty, snap decision. "It's usually you who starts these things. Come over here!" I find out later that, for once, the usual instigator was innocent. Ever yelled at a kid? I have. A long day, too much stress, or just tired. Whatever the reason, there's no excuse. Ever promised something and not come through? I have. It's not pleasant to see the look of hurt and disappointment in a kid's eyes. What I have to do—and I'm urging you to do the same—is humble myself and walk down the hallway to my child's room. I knock on the door and enter quietly. I gently and softly say, "Daddy was wrong. I made a mistake. I hurt you, and I'm sorry. Please forgive me." Then,

I make the situation right if I can. I make a change in the area where I blew it. Parenting should be a self-correcting process. Children will almost always forgive you when they see genuine sorrow and real change. If we expect them to be truly sorry and correct their mistakes, we'd better do the same.

Kiss the Lecture Good-Bye

Last, you need to realize that children and teens have very brief attention spans. Especially when parents are talking. Give up the lecture as a means of communication. I know it's a shame, because some of you are superb lecturers. You slowly build your case. Its logic is airtight. It's nothing less than a work of art. Perry Mason would cry with envy at your oratorical skills. Too bad your kid has tuned you out after the first minute. You're beating your gums for nothing.

Learn to speak in short, clear bursts. Most kids respond well to this approach. There are a few exceptions, but not many. Speaking in a brief, concise way shows respect. It's good communication, plus you can use the twenty minutes you would have wasted on a lecture to do something productive or fun. Now, if you have a kid who enjoys your lectures, fine. Go right ahead. I can see your kid with a pen and paper, taking careful notes. "What was Point Four, Dad, Mom?"

TWELVE

Who Am I, and What Am I Good At?

I will never forget a young man in his mid-twenties whom I saw in therapy a few years back. His family history was a nightmare. Both his parents were alcoholics who never showed any love for, or interest, in him. As far as they were concerned, he was a mistake. "You should never have been born," they told him over and over. These miserable excuses for parents told him many other vicious, critical things on a regular basis. The verbal abuse my client endured day after day from his mom and dad almost defied description. It was as if they systematically set out to destroy him. He could never please them. He was always a miserable failure in their eyes. They hated him, and he knew it.

By the time he reached elementary school, he had been stripped of his self-esteem. He hated himself just as much as his parents hated him. He was a very depressed, shy child who had no friends. He didn't have the courage to make friends. He was sure others would reject him. He had serious suicidal thoughts and was on the verge of killing himself. He believed he had no reason to live.

It was at his lowest and most desperate point that something wonderful happened. Something completely unexpected. Something that literally saved his life. A teacher recognized his musical ability and encouraged him to sing. This teacher saw what no one else had seen: This boy had talent in his voice. She arranged voice lessons, got him into several chorus groups, and pushed him to sing solos at school and her church.

As he told me about his teacher, tears streamed down his face. He was so grateful to her for giving him the gift of recognizing his musical ability. His singing became the central focus of his life. It gave him confidence and self-esteem that he'd never had. His parents didn't change. In fact, they continued to attack him verbally until he finally left home at the end of high school. But their power to destroy him was gone. He could sing, and they couldn't take that from him.

This story is an illustration of the powerful contribution competence makes to self-esteem. The only thing that kept this young man alive was his skill in singing. Even though he had nothing else that was positive in his life, his competence in music was enough to sustain him. Every child needs an area of competence. Without competence, healthy self-esteem will not develop.

The Best Anti-Sin Program

Competence is an ability or skill. It means being good at something. All children are asking themselves, "What am I good at? What can I really excel at?" It is absolutely vital that they find an answer. Your job as a parent is to help your kids answer this question and find something they can do well. If you fail to find your children a skill, their self-esteem will suffer. They will be much more likely to make mistakes that will cripple and damage their lives.

In my practice I see a lot of kids who are lazy. Unmotivated.

They're not putting forth much effort in school, in their activities, or in their spiritual lives. These kids are just coasting through life with an "I don't care" attitude. Their frustrated parents tell me their kids "just aren't achieving their full potential." Most of these kids are lazy because they have no area of competence. They're not good at anything, so they have no confidence. They're scared to fail, so they don't try.

I'll tell you what I tell their parents. You must find your child a skill and find it as quickly as you can. When your kid has a skill, he automatically has confidence in himself. This confidence is infectious and will spread to the other areas of his life. It will give him the courage to try hard in areas of weakness. "I'm good at baseball, so I can try at math. Even if I don't do well at math, that's okay, because I'm a good baseball player." You see how it works? When a kid can do something well—almost anything at all—he feeds off that strength. He now has the intestinal fortitude—the "guts"—to give other life experiences his best shot.

Kids who act out, get addicted, get pulled into crime, or get stuck in some other area of sin, often have not found an area of competence. It's easy to be good at drinking, drugs, stealing, sex, cheating, gambling. . . If your kid doesn't find an area of positive competence, he'll find an area of negative competence. I guarantee it! Your kid will find something he's good at. Something he can use to draw attention and approval from peers. You'd better make sure it's something positive.

I ask the kids who come to my office, "What are you good at?" Here are the answers I often get:

- "I go to the mall."
- "I hang out with my friends."

- "I talk on the phone."
- "I listen to music."
- "I watch TV."
- "I play computer games."

These are not areas of competence! If these kids aren't already involved in some area of sinful competence, they soon may be. The best anti-sin program I know is finding kids an area of competence. When they're good at a healthy activity, they don't need to be good at a sinful activity. Kids who discover a skill also discover motivation to work hard, protection from temptation, and a basis of self-esteem for life.

In Colossians, chapter 3, verse 23, God tells us how we are to live: "Whatever you do, work at it with all your heart, as working for the Lord, not for men." God is saying, do your very best. Don't be lazy. Strive for excellence. Do everything with Me in mind. Wow! This is exactly the way we want our kids to live, isn't it? How can we make this happen? I believe giving our kids the gift of competence is a central part of leading them into this kind of productive, God-centered lifestyle. Here are some practical action steps in the area of competence.

Every Kid Has a Talent

Tell your child that she has an ability. You never, ever waver in your confidence that there is an area in which she will excel. You might begin to wonder in your own mind, because the find-a-skill process takes longer with some kids. But you don't say, "Well, Susie, it doesn't look good. I'm not sure if you're good at anything." No! Here's what you say when frustration mounts:

"You've got an ability, Susie. I know it. We just have to find it."

God gives every person talents and gifts. In fact, at the point of becoming a Christian, each person receives a spiritual gift (1 Corinthians, chapter 12). We are also given human abilities, and it is our responsibility to use these abilities in the service of Christ (1 Peter 4:10–11). Your kid may doubt you when you say she has abilities. Direct her to the Bible. Then it's not you saying it; it's God who is saying it.

Go Ahead, Be Pushy

Find areas of interest and enjoyment, and push for involvement. There are times when it's necessary to push your kid, and this is one of them. If your child likes something, it just might lead to a skill. I'll never forget how my cruel, heartless parents pushed me into Little League baseball. I like baseball, so they signed me up on the Dodgers. On the way to my first practice, I got cold feet and told my mom I'd changed my mind. She said, "You'll be fine, kiddo." She stopped our big VistaCruiser station wagon at the practice field, pushed me out the door, and drove off in a cloud of dust. I was left standing there, holding my cap and glove. I didn't like my mother at that moment. Ten minutes later, I was having the time of my life. I learned how to play baseball, got to know a lot of guys my age, and had a great two years in Little League. All because my parents pushed me.

There are many activities you can push your kid into. Sports are a great avenue to skills. There are school teams and city leagues. Maybe your kid enjoys golf, tennis, or bowling. There are hobbies of all sorts: mechanics, woodworking, sewing, computers, crafts, etc. Look for interest in school subjects like math, science, literature, history, languages, and many more. Work with teachers and come up with creative ways to encourage your child to learn more in his favorite subject. You can sample the variety of extracurricular activities and clubs: scouting, music, drama, horseback riding, and dancing. There are activities of which most parents are not even aware.

Every single kid must be involved in some area of interest. Don't over-involve her, but she needs at least one interest. Let the kid choose, but she must choose something. Give it a decent trial, at least one month, to see if things will click. If it doesn't pan out, choose another activity and try again. It is completely unacceptable to allow a child to come home from school and do nothing except eat, watch television, and goof off. That is being a slug, and slugs find other slugs to hang out with, and they eventually get into trouble.

Sandy and I give feedback whenever we see a skill or a possible skill. We're low-key. We don't gush all over them. We don't want to apply too much pressure by being too interested in their being good at a particular activity. We're pushing Emily in singing, drama, and writing. Leeann has real ability in playing the piano and drawing. Nancy is being encouraged to develop her skills in drama, leadership, and piano. William has not yet started school, but he is gung ho into sports of all kinds. He shows real interest in golf now, so we're encouraging him to work on his skills in this greatest of all sports. (I know this will come as a huge shock, but William's dear old dad likes golf, too.)

The Total Truth

A major part of competence is knowing yourself. Your child needs to know who he is—strengths, weaknesses, blind spots, and personality traits—to be confident and have healthy self-esteem. How can he feel good about someone he doesn't know? God wants your child to have an honest and accurate picture of himself or herself:

> *For by the grace given me I say to every one of you:*
> *Do not think of yourself more highly than you ought,*
> *but rather think of yourself with sober judgment,*
> *in accordance with the measure of faith God has given you.*
> ROMANS 12:3

To help your child paint this accurate self-portrait, you must consistently give her the truth about herself in all areas. Across the board. I've already covered the importance of feedback concerning skills and abilities. Just be realistic. Don't lie or exaggerate. If she can't sing, she can't sing! I've seen parents encourage their child to be a soloist when it's painfully obvious she doesn't have the pipes.

This accurate view of self also includes weaknesses. Your child has weaknesses and must learn how to deal with them. Handle these areas very carefully and in private. Don't say, "You're terrible at that." Instead, say, "That's not one of your strong points, Bobby." Some weaknesses, like in a particular sport, don't need to be worked on or corrected. You'll just direct your child to a sport or activity in which he can enjoy success. Other weak areas, like personality traits, will need to be addressed. Character is important, so you'll work with your child to help him be aware of, and change, negative aspects of his personality.

Help Your Kid Be Christlike

One of the essential functions parents have is developing character in their children. Specifically, Christlike character. It's vital that children see themselves as being like Christ. This is, without question, the centerpiece of an accurate view of self and the source of true competence. The good news is, we parents can create character in our kids. One of the ways we can do this is to reinforce Christlike behavior when we see it.

Some time ago, we were all sitting at the dining room table at the start of supper. I cut my prayer short because Sandy had made sourdough rolls. I love sourdough rolls. I would kill for sourdough rolls. Anyway, the sourdough rolls began their trip around the table. With four kids, it took a while. My anticipation grew as the basket approached the end of the table, where Emily and I were sitting. Emily took the basket, lifted the cloth, and paused. I was horrified to see that there was only one roll left! I couldn't believe it. Sandy had apparently made only five sourdough rolls. What kind of game was she playing?

It was an awkward moment. Then Emily, sweet Emily, said, "Dad, go ahead. You can take the last roll. I know you like sourdough rolls." I didn't waste any time. I grabbed that roll, and said, "Thanks, Emily. That was very kind." Later that evening, just before bed, I made it a point to thank Emily again for her act of kindness. I told her that she was like Christ in being a kind, thoughtful servant. Sandy told me later: "You know, you could have broken the roll in half and shared it with Emily." I said, "Yeah. I could have. But I wanted to give Emily a chance to be like Christ." Actually, that didn't dawn on me. I just wanted that roll. I was being kind—like Christ—because I didn't say to Sandy what I wanted to say: "You could have made six rolls!"

As I did with Emily, look for situations in which your kids display positive and Christlike qualities. Catch them being like Christ, and verbally stroke them:

- "You're friendly."
- "You're sensitive to the needs of others."
- "You speak the truth."
- "You're kind."
- "You didn't quit."
- "You chose to forgive."
- "You shared with your sister."
- "You read the Bible."
- "You love Jesus, and it shows."

Your children will take your objective feedback and use it to form their identities. Step by step, positive reinforcement by positive reinforcement, you will help mold them into being like Christ.

Networking for Your Kid

Have other adults in your child's life also provide feedback on abilities and personal qualities: family members, friends, teachers, coaches, pastors, and youth leaders. Ask these persons to communicate directly to your child the positive qualities they observe. They can do it verbally or in writing.

I can remember the personal notes my private school

teachers wrote to me at the end of each grading period. It was school policy, and I'm glad it was. I couldn't wait to read those notes! I devoured them. My teachers commented on my academic work and my personality. The praise I received for my self-discipline, sense of humor, and writing ability helped shape my life.

In just these past two weeks, here's the feedback our kids got from other key adults in their lives. I spoke to Josie Reed, Emily's language arts teacher. Josie told me she's seen these qualities in Emily: maturity, a caring spirit, a love for God, and real leadership ability. Did I keep this information to myself? No way. I went home and told Emily exactly what Josie had said. My dad e-mailed Emily and thanked her for her kind note to him. He told her she was a caring person.

Sandy spoke to several of Leeann's teachers and was told she is attentive, does quality work, shows respect, does well socially, and she's a joy to have in class. Sandy gave this feedback directly to Leeann. John and Connie Hoffman, good friends, also gave us feedback on Leeann. Leeann, who is very good friends with their daughter Ashley, had spent the night at their home. John and Connie told us Leeann was a great kid: friendly, obedient, and caring. We passed on this feedback to Leeann.

Gail Gray, one of the all-time great teachers, has Nancy in her third-grade class. Gail, who is a lot like Nancy, told us Nancy is "the perfect kid." She described Nancy as industrious, smart, blunt in her speaking style, and honest, with a great personality. We told Nancy what Gail had said, with the exception of the "perfect kid" comment. We don't want Nancy's head to get too big.

William got his positive feedback from three great guys:

Corky Tatum, Steve Powell, and Rocky Glisson. All three came by the house, watched William playing golf, and praised him for his golfing skills. Steve, a neighbor and a great pastor, made this unnecessary comment to me: "That kid is better than you at golf." Steve noticed that William had hit his balls closer to our target than I had. What he said was true, but not really necessary. Of course, I let it pass because it made William feel great.

Encouraging other adults to reinforce your child's positive qualities adds a powerful dimension to your program of building Christlike character. These persons see parts of your child that you don't see. In the case of teachers, they spend more time with your kid than you do. Also, feedback packs more punch when it comes from someone else. Kids, especially teenagers, tend to discount what parents say. Teens think you really don't know them, you're wrong most of the time, and, "Oh, you're my parent. You're supposed to say that." When other adults make comments to teens, they sit up and take notice.

THIRTEEN

My Identity in Christ

The Real Equalizer

A few years ago, there was a neat television show called *The Equalizer*. It told the stories—fictional, of course—of persons who were in desperate situations. These poor souls were at the end of their ropes. Surrounded by bad guys. At the brink of personal, family, or financial ruin. Sometimes, their very lives were at stake. When these individuals had run out of options and had no one else to turn to, they called the Equalizer.

The Equalizer was Robert McCall, a fiftyish man played by the excellent English character actor, Edward Woodward. Mr. McCall offered his special services to anyone who couldn't handle a crisis situation on his or her own. He called himself the Equalizer because he more than made up for the unequal odds his clients faced. He leveled the playing field. Mr. McCall was cool. Clint Eastwood cool. He was unbelievably well dressed. He had an amazing collection of expensive, three-piece suits. He was incredibly skilled in firearms, hand-to-hand combat, picking locks, explosive devices, choosing the right bottle of champagne, plumbing, psychological gamesmanship, and every other area needed to do battle with mean, nasty criminals. He was in control. He hardly broke a sweat. He knew no fear. Of course, he always outfought and defeated the bad guys. At the end of every show, the Equalizer saved the poor, helpless victims from certain destruction.

I've got some bad news for you. Very bad news. While *The*

Equalizer was just a television show, it is an eerily accurate illustration of the evil forces operating in the life of your child. Your child is the helpless victim at the mercy of a real-life bad guy. A bad guy with tremendous power and cunning. This bad guy's name is Satan. Make no mistake. Satan is real and he hates your kid's guts. He's got a picture of your kid tacked up on the bulletin board in hell. He's holding regular strategy meetings on how to get to your kid. If Satan can't have your kid's soul, he'll settle for whatever damage he can do in his life. He knows your kid's weaknesses and he'll attack at those vulnerable points. Satan loves to go after kids because he has the opportunity to put into place sinful, destructive patterns that can last a lifetime.

You don't believe me? Read the chilling words in 1 Peter 5:8:

> *Be self-controlled and alert.*
> *Your enemy the devil prowls around*
> *like a roaring lion looking for*
> *someone to devour.*

Well, that's the bad news. I have some good news, as well. Very good news. In 1 Peter 5:9 we are given the answer to dealing with Satan:

> *Resist him, standing firm in the faith,*
> *because you know that your brothers*
> *throughout the world are undergoing*
> *the same kind of sufferings.*

Frankly, your kid doesn't have a chance, alone, against Satan. But she doesn't have to face Satan alone. Your children can resist Satan by "standing firm in the faith." Faith in what, or whom? Faith in the real Equalizer, God Himself. God will come and stand by your child. He'll protect her. Comfort her. Guide her. Give her strength to stand up to Satan. In the verse immediately preceding the warning about Satan, are the encouraging words, *"Cast all your anxiety on him* because he *cares for you"* (1 Peter 5:7; italics mine).

Your child needs God to win the war against Satan. Your child also needs God for genuine self-esteem. There is no authentic, complete self-esteem apart from a relationship with God. All humans are made for a relationship with God, and we can see ourselves as worthy only when we are connected to Him.

We have worth because God created us:

> *I praise you because I am fearfully*
> *and wonderfully made;*
> *your works are wonderful,*
> *I know that full well.*
> PSALM 139:14

We have worth because God loves us so much that He sent Jesus Christ to die for us on the cross:

> *"For God so loved the world that*
> *he gave his one and only Son,*
> *that whoever believes in him*
> *shall not perish but have eternal life."*
> JOHN 3:16

Bring Your Child to Christ

Parents, the first thing you must do is to make sure your child is connected to God. It can be pretty tough to figure out how to do this, with all the conflicting messages about God and spirituality out there. There is a high degree of interest in "spiritual" things these days, and the media is crammed full of all kinds of ideas on how to be spiritual. Harness the "power within." Call the psychic hot line. Find out what past lives you've lived. Follow Allah. Follow the teachings of Buddha. Discover God in a tree or a mountain. Talk to an angel. Just be a good person. And on and on. Most of these so-called spiritual advisors agree on one thing: There are many ways to find "God."

As my youngest daughter Nancy would say, "Let's cut to the chase." The truth, as always, is found in the Bible. As a matter of fact, there is only one way to reach God and establish a relationship with Him. Jesus answered:

> *"I am the way and the truth and the life.*
> *No one comes to the Father except through me."*
> JOHN 14:6

That's absolutely black and white, isn't it? If you come across any spiritual approach that does not teach Jesus Christ as the only way to God, throw it out. It's worthless. Worse than that, it's dangerous because it will get you nowhere near God. It will get you near Satan, and you don't want that—for you or your child.

It can be hard for younger kids to understand the good news about Jesus Christ. They have a tough time grasping His death on the cross and what it means. When you say "invite Jesus into your heart," and "give Jesus your life," your child may not know what you're talking about. Try an approach that focuses on punishment. Kids understand being punished for bad things they do. Tell your child that Jesus took her punishment for all the things she has done wrong. "God loves you so much, He sent Jesus to take your punishment." She will understand that.

My pastor, Kirk Johnston, told a story from the pulpit that got my attention. I think it's an excellent way to explain to kids what Jesus did for them. A father was just having fits with his young son. The boy disobeyed time and time again. The dad tried everything, but the boy continued to act out. Finally, the dad took his son to a room and closed the door. He took off his belt and said it was time for some serious punishment. The kid began to cringe and whimper. Then the dad handed the belt to the boy and told the child to whip him! The boy resisted and said he couldn't do that. But the dad insisted. He took off his shirt and had his son whip him repeatedly and with force across his back. The boy was sobbing as he struck the blows. Then, when the son could no longer continue, his dad said, "That's enough." The dad then told his boy how Jesus took his punishment, just like he had taken his son's punishment.

When you bring your child to God through believing in Jesus Christ, he has the real Equalizer on his side. Trusting Jesus provides the most important ingredient in the building of his self-esteem. Knowing Christ is the initial, once-for-all step in establishing a relationship with God, with entering His "forever family." But in the Christian life it is only the beginning. There is another step that is an integral part of God's plan for us. The second step begins what is a lifelong process.

Help Your Child Grow in Christ

A key part of meeting your child's need for spirituality is helping her grow in Christ. Your goal is to guide your child to move from dependence on you to dependence on Christ. How do you do this? The main way is to show your child your dependence on Christ.

Do what I'm trying to do. I'm working hard to show my

kids that Jesus Christ isn't just a part of my life. He is all of my life. I don't limit Christ to church on Sundays, to Wednesday night prayer meeting, to praying before meals, and to times of crisis. I want my kids to see that Christ is an integral part of everything I do. Jesus Christ is my crutch, and I'm proud of it. I need Him every minute of every day. I tell my kids each evening how Christ guided me that day. How He met my needs. How, when I prayed to God through Christ, my prayers were answered. If I don't tell them these daily spiritual experiences, they won't realize how important Christ is to me. They'll assume I don't need Him every day. And if Dad doesn't need Christ every day, why should they?

Do what my dad did when I was growing up. My dad is the most godly man I know. He had the most impact on my spiritual life of anyone in my childhood. That's because he was my dad. If I can follow, and if you can follow, Bill Clarke's spiritual building program, we'll be doing all we can to help our kids grow in Christ. I say "program" because it was a program. Everything my dad did spiritually he did by design. He wanted to grow spiritually himself, and he wanted my brother Mark and me to grow spiritually. My dad repeatedly told Mark and me: "There's nothing more important in life than a vital, growing relationship with Jesus Christ." But he didn't just say it. He took action to make it happen in our lives.

My dad modeled a godly lifestyle. He had a relationship with Jesus Christ that worked. I wanted a relationship with Christ like the one he had. One of the vivid memories etched in my mind is of my dad in his chair in the family room, every morning of my life, having his devotions. He had the Bible open, plus a few other books: Bible study aids, devotional guides, etc. Every morning, without fail. I could count on Dad doing his devotions like the sun coming up. Even when I got up at different times—weekends, holidays—Dad would be there. I finally figured out years later that Dad made sure I saw him, no matter when I got up. I guess Dad figured if I saw him having his quiet time with God every morning, I'd realize how important God was to him. Maybe I'd be motivated to develop my own quiet time as an adult. Right on both counts. I have a daily quiet time, and I want my kids to see me doing it.

Dad talked a lot about his spiritual life. Hardly a day went by when he didn't share with Mark and me some spiritual tidbit from his day. God did this. God did that. I've prayed about this issue, and God answered today. I talked to a man about Christ this morning, and he became a Christian. Listen to what I learned in my Bible study this morning. I met with some men from church for lunch and we talked about how God is leading each of us in unique ways. Man! I got the impression all my dad thought about all day was God.

My dad led a once-a-week family devotional time. It wasn't too long. Just twenty or thirty minutes. He was always prepared and had something to teach. He didn't just show up and wing it. He taught briefly from the Bible, shared personally, and added a practical application. We always prayed at the end. When I was a teenager, with a rotten attitude during devotions, he tolerated me. I didn't want to be there, and the whole world knew it. My dad didn't let it bother him. He just kept on going. I look back now with fond memories of those devotional meetings. It wasn't just what I learned that made a difference in my life. It was Dad's rock-solid faithfulness week in and week out that impressed me. Unless the house burned down, we were going to have devotions once a week in that family room.

My dad was a praying man. I saw him pray silently during

his morning quiet time. He prayed before every family meal. He prayed in church. He prayed during family devotions. He prayed with me privately at bedtime. He told me he prayed for me every day—and I believed him. When my dad prayed, you just knew God was listening. His prayers were real and honest and open. They were the prayers of a man who really knew the God he was talking to. I mean, it was like they were best of friends. He could say anything to God. He loved God, and you knew, just knew, that God loved him.

Dad kept Mark and me in a good children's ministry and a good youth group. He and Mom knew the leaders and what was being taught. He talked to my Sunday school teachers to find out their impressions of me and my spiritual life. I'm afraid in junior high and senior high school, he didn't get many good reports. I hated youth group with a passion. I had a few friends there, but I wasn't too popular. I was popular at secular school and was interested only in spending time with my school buddies. I tried to get out of going to youth group, with no success. My dad made me go and didn't apologize for it. He told me he wanted me to learn about Jesus Christ, be around other Christian kids, be involved in healthy activities, and emulate the godly youth leaders. I thought he was crazy. I thought he was out of touch.

Turns out, Dad was right again. That youth group, despite my pitiful attitude, was good for me. Frank Couch, one of my youth pastors, was a terrific guy and a great model. I wouldn't admit it, but I did have a lot of fun playing soccer and other games with the youth group. More than anything, it kept me connected to Jesus Christ. Even though at times it was a very fragile connection, it was enough to get me through some difficult, confusing stretches in my life.

FOURTEEN

Cut the Apron Strings, and Let Me Go

"I Want My Life Back"

I have a dream. A wild, crazy, impossible dream. I dream that one day all my children will grow up and leave. My home will be mine again. I'll be able to walk around in my underwear. I'll be able to sleep in. I'll have some closet space for my clothes. I'll be able to sit in my favorite chair anytime I want. My life will be mine again. I'll have free time! I'll do what I want to do. I'll play golf. I'll goof off. I'll read books. I'll sit and stare at the wall if I feel like it. I'll be selfish again. I miss being selfish.

My food will be mine again. The leftovers from a great meal will be mine. All mine! Never again will I have to fight my way to the refrigerator through a herd of permanently hungry, carnivorous, herbivorous (actually, they eat anything) savages—only to find the shelves stripped bare of all edible food. Cottage cheese, low-fat yogurt, and mayonnaise don't count. I will no longer have to endure fast-food places. (I won't use the term "restaurants"!) I will not be tortured again by the long lines, always being served by the "new" counter person, the food that tastes like cardboard, fighting to get my kid the special toy she'll discard after ten minutes, the deafening decibel level, and the perennially sticky seats and tables.

My peace of mind and personal space will be mine again. It will be quiet in my home. I'll be able to actually think for minutes at a time without interruptions. I'll have my first complete thought in years. I'll do things around the home without my every move being watched. People made a big deal of that television show a few years ago when a family allowed a film crew to film everything they did in the home for a full year. What's the big deal? That's how I've lived for years! My children are always around. Unlike pets, you can't just toss them in the backyard with a water dish and a bowl of last night's leftovers. I can't do anything alone. I haven't gone to the bathroom alone in thirteen years! There's always a little person standing there, staring at me.

But, best of all, my wife will be mine again. I'm tired of sharing her. I want her back, all to myself. Sandy was the original model, and she is still the best. When all the kids have moved out, it's going to be time for Sandy and me to have fun. To make up for lost time. And I don't mean playing Canasta or working in the garden. After all, one of the main reasons you help your children achieve physical and emotional independence is this: to get the kids out of the house so you can have some fun!

There are two other good reasons. One, you fulfill your ultimate goal as a parent: to raise your kids in order to prepare them to live on their own. Two, you meet the last need required for healthy self-esteem. Have you ever met a dependent person with a confident, positive view of self? Of course not. You never will.

One of the most pathetic sights I see in counseling is the dependent young adult. He has not achieved independence from his parents. He can't make it in the world on his own. He still relies heavily on his parents for emotional, perhaps even financial support. Often, he still lives at home. My goal in this kind of case is twofold: get the parents to let go, and teach the young person the tools of independent living. It's not easy work. The dependent person has seriously low self-esteem and very little confidence to face the world without the parental safety net. To make sure your kid doesn't end up like this, follow these steps.

"Make Your Own Decisions"

Allow your children to make their own decisions whenever possible. If it isn't a critical area—life or death—let them decide. It's good practice. They can decide which clothes they buy and wear, as long as what they choose is appropriate. They choose which activity they want to do on the weekend. They choose which friends to ask over to the house. They choose what to order in a restaurant. The only rule is, they're stuck with what they order. If they don't like their food, tough.

With younger kids, offer them choices. William, who's four, is not quite old enough to pick out his own clothes. He'd choose some hideous combination and probably put on two different colored socks. Plus, he's a little overwhelmed by all the choices and has trouble making up his mind. We show him two outfits and say, "Do you want to wear this one or that one?" He makes a choice and feels good about himself. He's Mr. Independent. We use the same approach when it comes to chores: "Do you want to pick up your toys or set the table?"

In these noncritical areas, we use language that encourages independence:

- "The choice is yours."
- "You decide about that."
- "It's your decision."
- "It's up to you."

- "Do what you believe you should do."
- "Think about it, then make the call."

When you talk this way, you build your children's confidence in their ability to make decisions. You send the message: "You're a sharp kid, and we know you are capable of making good choices in life." Make sure they realize they'll make mistakes. Everybody does. That's part of the learning process in life.

Force your kids to wrestle with tough decisions. When your kids come to you with problems and sticky situations, don't immediately give them an answer. Even if you're right, they don't learn anything. They don't learn to think for themselves. I have clients whose parents fed them answers all through childhood. When life got rough, they'd run to Mommy and Daddy and get the solution. Now, these clients are incredibly indecisive. They're totally paralyzed when faced with decisions. They'll call twenty persons, get advice from each, and still not know what to do.

When your kids approach you with issues, always ask them, "What do you think?" Make them struggle with the situation out loud and think their way through it. Give your input, but only after they have used their own brain cells to arrive at a decision. If it isn't a vital area, let them go ahead with their decision. Even if it's a mistake. Some of life's most important lessons are learned from mistakes.

Show your kids how you make decisions. No one else is going to teach them how. That's your job. Let them see you: listing the pros and cons, praying, reading the Bible, talking to your spouse, talking to family members and good friends, and getting counsel from trusted persons. Too many parents keep their decision making a secret. Those parents tell me, "We don't want to scare our kids or make them insecure." My response is, "If you don't show them how to make decisions now, they'll be scared and insecure when they hit the real world."

Whatever skill you don't teach your kids is a skill they won't have when they're adults. Many clients tell me: "I never saw my parents argue. If they did, it was behind closed doors." Guess what these clients have no idea how to do? Right. They don't know how to deal with conflict. I don't blame them. Nobody showed them. I teach them how to fight fair and how to resolve conflicts, but it would have saved a lot of pain and damage if their parents had done the job. The same principle is true of decision making. Let your kids see the behind-the-scenes steps you take to make choices in life. You'll be doing them a huge favor.

Stand Up for Christ

If your kids are Christians, then a major part of their independence is standing up for Jesus Christ. If they are public and not private Christians, they will build their faith and be truly independent. Jesus' words recorded in Matthew 5:16 are great to use in teaching:

> *"In the same way, let your light shine before men,*
> *that they may see your good deeds*
> *and praise your Father in heaven."*

I'm proud to say my kids are letting their light shine. Emily had a school assignment to write about what job she would like to do for a day. Her chosen topic was: "I was a missionary for a day." Dad and Mom were thrilled. I wouldn't have had the guts to do that as a kid. Leeann chose not to go to a sleepover because she found out some morally questionable girls were going to be there. Nancy called us one time from a sleepover to ask if she could watch a certain movie her friend had selected. She didn't care what her friend or her parents thought. She wasn't going to risk compromising her Christian principles. Plus, if we found out, she knew she'd be in big trouble.

The Law of the Playground

The world is a nasty place. You know that. And it's getting nastier all the time. And nowhere is it nastier than in your child's world. The deterioration of our culture and the breakdown of the family are producing more and more problem kids. There are a lot of bullies, creeps, and just plain mean kids out there. They enjoy teasing, taunting, and physically beating up other children. These vicious juvenile delinquents are everywhere: public schools, Christian schools, churches, day care centers, and neighborhoods. I'm not talking just about boys. Girls can be incredibly catty and brutal. Your child will come into contact with these kids. Guaranteed. The only question is: How will your child deal with these bullies?

Parents, you've got to get your kids ready to meet the punks of this world. All kids need to be prepared, but there are certain categories of children who are in particular need of anti-punk training: only children, sensitive children, passive children, shy children, children with disabilities, children with speech problems, and children who haven't had much exposure to kids of the same sex. These kids need to be toughened up so they can deal effectively with the attacks of their peers.

You've already read part of my program for preparation. Meeting the four needs I've covered up to now—love, respect, competence, and spirituality—will toughen your kids and give them a healthy level of confidence. Here are some more ideas. First, let siblings tease each other, and do not intervene unless it gets out of hand. Good old, run-of-the-mill teasing helps your kids build up tolerance. It's good practice for the real thing. So let your kids learn how to take it and dish it out in interactions with their brothers and sisters. If you protect your children from these family attacks, you'll create a bunch of little Lord Fauntleroys. They'll be cut to ribbons out there where it's really tough.

Second, expose your kids to peers of the same sex in the neighborhood, at school, and in church. These days, it's important to get your children used to interacting with peers at a young age. The more social skills your children have before they hit school, the better. Third, talk specifically to your kids about what they're going to face. They're going into battle and they might as well know it. Discuss the broad range of possible verbal insults—body characterizations, their name, paternity, family heritage, etc. Develop strategies and role-play situations.

What do you do when your kid is being attacked, verbally or physically, on a regular basis? The bottom line is: Do not allow your child to passively endure vicious teasing or physical bullying. If your child fails to respond, her self-esteem and independence will be seriously wounded. I've had many parents, usually moms, tell me: "But my child should turn the other cheek, like it says in the Bible. Wouldn't Jesus want that?" I reply: "If your child continues to allow bullying, she'll invite more intense bullying. She could be emotionally crippled for life. Would Jesus want that?"

I tell parents that kids are like a group of sharks in the ocean. When one of them bleeds, they all attack without mercy until there's nothing left of the victim. The sad reality is, even the good, decent kids join in the massacre. That's not right. That's not fair. But that's the way it is. I believe there is a place for assertiveness in the lives of Christian adults and kids. Ephesians 4:26 instructs us: "In your anger do not sin." Let's look at some practical ways you can teach your child to be angry, stop the bullying, and not sin in the process.

Step One is to stay out of it. It's the absolute kiss of death to have Mommy or Daddy directly intervene. It won't stop the bullying, and it will humiliate your child. Unless there is a clear threat of serious physical harm, just work with your child behind the scenes.

Step Two is to teach your child to show no weakness. This will be tough if your kid is the sensitive type, but it's critical to success. Practice and role-play until your kid can stare back at you and show no visible response. He, or she, has to fake a calm exterior and stuff all feelings. When your kid comes home, he can pour out his heart and cry and be as pitiful as he wants to be. But not in front of the bully. That is no place for honest expression: "You've hurt my feelings, Bubba." No! That's what Bubba and all bullies want: a reaction.

Step Three is to train your child in the art of verbal comebacks. Ignoring insults usually doesn't work. Your child can try it, but don't get your hopes up. What usually does work is calm, witty, sometimes humorous, and sarcastic replies to the bully's taunts. Don't recommend any foul language or vicious retorts. That wouldn't be Christlike. Help your child come up with a collection of memorized comebacks that will make him more of a challenge to the bully. Bullies like easy marks and don't typically have the stomach for a prolonged match of wits. They don't want to risk looking bad in front of their peers. Check with other parents to find some good, contemporary comebacks. Have your kid ask his friends for some material. "Your mother wears army boots" probably won't work in this day and age. Again, role-play until your kid can zing you back with his snappy one-liners.

Step Four is to advise your kid to get some support from friends. If even one kid will agree to back him up, chances are better the bully will back off. It's harder to pick on two kids. If your child's friend has a smart mouth and is good at verbal jousting, so much the better. In fact, the steps I've suggested are designed to gather support from the peers observing the bullying. Bullies always play to the crowd. If your kid's responses impress even a few of the onlookers, the bully is in trouble. When the bully senses a loss of even a little crowd support, he'll move on to another kid.

Step Five is the judicious use of retaliatory physical measures. In other words, there may come a time when your kid has to throw a punch. You make it clear that your child is to strike back only in self-defense. He is never to throw the first punch. I've taught my kids that if any kid hits them, they are allowed to hit back to protect themselves. I do not want one of my kids to be beaten like a drum and not respond. Sometimes, a physical confrontation cannot be avoided. Even if your kid loses the fight, at least he goes down swinging. That may make him too tough an opponent for the bully. And it will win him some respect and support from the ringside crowd.

One final point. When a bully tells your kid to meet him after school for a fight, there's only one good response: "No, let's do it right now." The bully wants to get mileage all day out of his challenge. He wants your kid to suffer in anguish for hours. But most of all, he wants no school officials around to stop the fight and punish him. When your kid forces the bully to fight immediately, it ensures that the fight won't go the distance. If a teacher shows up, the bully may get in trouble. Plus, your kid earns some respect from other peers.

Push Them out of the Nest

Your kids will not become independent unless you push them into healthy activities away from home. Don't let them become too comfortable at home, because they won't be living there forever. As I stated in chapter 2, sleepovers ought to begin in second grade. Unless your child has a bona fide emergency or some extraordinary crisis, make her stay the night. If a little whining brings Mom or Dad running to rescue her, she may never complete a sleepover.

I'm a big believer in Christian summer camps. Check out the camp and the leaders carefully. Because your kids will be out of your care for at least one week, you must demand the highest possible caliber of Christianity in the camp administration and counselors. Sandy and I have been delighted with the Pioneer Camping Ministry and Camp Cherith here in Florida. Some of the finest Christians we've ever met run this ministry. Our girls have had fun, matured in many areas, and grown spiritually as a result of their camp experiences.

Church youth outings and events are a part of building independence in your kids. If they don't want to go, tough. Hear them out, listen and reflect, then tell them to get in the car. School activities and sports are a good social outlet and foster independence. At fifteen or sixteen years of age, a part-time job is a possibility. The job must be earned with good grades and good behavior. Also, the hours must be limited. Any more than ten to twelve hours a week is a mistake. It will lead to fatigue, lower grades, and a reduced social life.

Teach Money Management

You can't live without money. And you can't live too well if you don't know how to handle your money. Frankly, this was a weak area of my life until my mid-twenties. Just to prove my parents weren't perfect, they didn't teach me a great deal about money. Looking back, they were probably too generous. I had to learn the nuts and bolts of money management as an adult.

To prepare your kids for the financial realities of life, model careful budgeting and use of your money. Show them the bills. Show them your budget. Tell them how much you make each month and how much you spend. Teach them how to balance a checkbook. At least by the end of junior high, your kids ought to have a firm grasp on these money skills. Model tithing to the church and other Christian ministries. Make it clear that all your money is God's money. He has provided it to meet your needs. It's only right and biblical to give back a portion of what God has given so generously. If you want your kids to give to God, let them see you doing it.

Pay your kids for certain jobs they do around the home. When they have some money, you can teach them how to manage it. I like this approach: spend, save, and share—the three s's (this is not original with me). Your kids can spend a certain percentage of their money, save a certain percentage, and share a certain percentage with the Lord. Younger kids need to pay a small percentage of birthday gifts for family and friends. Also, they ought to chip in a little for toys they want. Nothing is free, and they need to realize this at a young age. Your kid wants the top-of-the-line athletic shoes? Great! He can cough up part of the price tag. As your kids move into junior high and beyond, require them to pay a percentage of their expenses: car, gas, insurance, clothes, entertainment. . . . They'll scream in pain, but they'll learn the value of money.

Teach Basic Living Skills

Before your kids leave home, you need to train them in some humdrum but fundamental areas. They need to know how to do basic household cleaning. A magic genie (or Mom) will not clean their toilets for them when they're living in their own places. They've got to learn how to cook. Boys *and* girls! I'm not talking about gourmet meals. Just simple, hearty fare. They need to be able to do their own laundry. By junior high, your kids should be doing some of their own laundry every week. And one other thing: Kids must master the skill of taking care of a car. This is especially important with the old rattletraps they'll be driving for a while. Understanding the way an engine works, changing the oil every three thousand miles, and doing regular maintenance will save them thousands of dollars.

Healthy self-esteem is critical to a successful life. But it won't just happen. You, as the parent, make it happen. Make whatever changes you need to make in your life to meet these five needs—love, respect, competence, spirituality, and independence. Because if you consistently meet these five needs, your children will develop healthy self-esteem. They'll have better relationships. They'll be more successful in life. Best of all, they'll be closer to God.

FIFTEEN

Who's in Charge? Discipline That Works!

Parenthood Ain't Pretty

You're at the mall with your children. It's just you and them—no spouse. You've just said no to your little boy. Without warning, he suddenly throws himself to the floor and launches into a full-blown tantrum. I mean, this tantrum has it all: yelling and screaming, foaming at the mouth, legs and arms thrashing, and the little back arched. If it weren't so annoying, you'd be impressed with his acrobatic ability. But it is annoying. . .and embarrassing.

You see disapproving looks from several bystanders, and you get the distinct impression they blame you for your son's behavior. You lean down to grab his arm, he jerks up suddenly, and his head connects with your head. Your head is ringing, your arms are full of bags, and you want to spank Timmy so badly you can taste it. It's ten miles to the parking lot. What do you do?

Here's another example. It's bedtime at your home. At last! It's been a long day and even though you love your kids, you've had about enough. You want peace and quiet, and some time for yourself. You want your kids to go to bed, go to sleep, and leave you alone. That's the dream. The reality is, you have one child who won't go to bed. Tonight, like most nights, she fights bedtime tooth and nail. She keeps dragging out of her room with the same ridiculous excuses: "I'm thinking bad thoughts." "I need water"—which, of course, is followed five minutes later by, "I have to go to the bathroom." Oh, what a shocker! "I heard a strange noise." And the classic: "It's too dark in here." You say, "Funny thing, honey. It gets dark every night about this same time."

You try all the same ridiculous solutions: reasoning with her, threatening her, and begging her. You turn off all the lights. You lie down next to her in bed, which puts you to sleep, not her. You play music tapes. If you hear Aladdin, Little Mermaid, Raffi, or VeggieTales one more time you'll scream. Nothing works. It's 8:30, 9:00, 9:30, and another evening is shot. How do you get the kid to bed?

All right, here's yet another scene. Your thirteen-year-old daughter has just finished another one of her screaming, crying, whining tirades. All you did was ask her to hang up the phone because an hour and a half was enough time to talk. She didn't take it well. She said she hated you, that you didn't love her, and that you weren't "cool" like Cindy's mom. According to her, living with you is like being in a concentration camp. Your sweet, kind, obedient daughter has turned into a teenage werewolf.

Ever since her thirteenth birthday, it's been like an alien has invaded her body. She's angry, disrespectful, selfish, critical, and lies like a rug. At least she isn't moody. She has only one mood: bad. She doesn't want much. Just complete freedom, all your money, and everything her way. What do you do with a teenager like this? (And most of them are like this.)

The Solution Is Discipline

These are just three scenes. I could go on and on. I have four kids, and I have worked with a lot of parents and kids. All of us as parents have unpleasant stories like these, don't we? The problem in each one of these stories is a child:

- testing a parent;
- challenging authority;
- seeing how far he can go to get his way.

The solution is: discipline. Solid, healthy, balanced discipline. Discipline is the painful process of teaching children limits.

We must teach discipline because it leads to self-control, patience, character, respect, and accomplishment. Our children need these qualities to have a successful life. We discipline our kids for the same reasons God disciplines us.

> *Our fathers disciplined us*
> *for a little while as they thought best;*
> *but God disciplines us for our good,*
> *that we may share in his holiness.*
> *No discipline seems pleasant at the time, but painful.*
> *Later on, however, it produces a harvest of righteousness*
> *and peace for those who have been trained by it.*
> HEBREWS 12:10–11

We also teach discipline for ourselves, because if we don't, our children will make our lives a living nightmare. There's no end to the pain and damage undisciplined kids can wreak on our lives. Just look at poor old Eli and the horrible mess his sons Hophni and Phinehas made. To be sure, I don't have all the answers in the area of discipline. But I do have a training program—a strategy—that I believe will help you. My strategy begins with the three prerequisites for effective discipline. You must understand these three things first to have any chance of being an effective disciplinarian.

Your Children Need to Rebel

That's right. You read those words correctly. Rebellion is a healthy, normal, and important part of becoming one's own person, breaking away, and achieving independence. Your children won't become independent unless they rebel. You're thinking, *You're saying we can't stop it?* That's what I am saying. The key is to allow rebellion in minor areas, not major ones.

In my opinion, here are some minor areas: Hair is minor. Believe me. Let them wear their hair the way they want. It's really not a big deal. Some parents think long hair is one step away from drug use. It's not! It's just long hair. The kids' overall appearance is also not something to have a fit about. Within reason, let them wear the clothes they want to wear. Let them make a statement. There's no harm in this kind of "rebellion." And food. Don't force them to eat their vegetables. Don't force them to clean their plates. They'll eat when they're hungry. Very few kids starve to death. Now, if they choose not to eat the good food, there is a small price to pay. They can't have snacks or dessert.

All you moms get ready to hear something you're not going to like. I'm about to break a lot of hearts. Their rooms are also a minor area. Please, stop trying to make your kids clean their rooms. Oh, the vicious, pitched battles I've seen over the condition of the rooms! It's not worth it! Let them revel in their own filth, disorder, and clutter! It's a safe expression of rebellion. Let it go, like releasing a dove to the heavens. Now, if you see a rat squeezing out the door of the room, you may have a real problem. If men in those white environmental suits come to your front door, you'll know you'll probably have to take steps.

If you win in these areas, your kids will rebel in other, major areas. I've seen a lot of acting-out kids whose hair is short and whose rooms are clean and tidy. They've simply moved on to dangerous areas of rebellion. Would you rather have your kids rebel with a messy room or by getting involved in drugs or sex? That could very well be your choice!

Major areas of rebellion are: alcohol, drugs, sex, breaking laws, lying, disrespect, and hanging out with dangerous kids. You fight these battles with all you've got, because these behaviors can destroy your child. I urge zero tolerance in these areas. Prioritize and fight only the battles that are worth fighting. If you respond to every behavior you disagree with, you'll be a basket case! And your kid will rebel big-time in the big areas.

You Cannot Control Your Children's Behavior

You are doomed to lose the battle for control over your children's behavior. You can't control the behavior of any other person! Think about it. Can you control your spouse's behavior? Of course not. I hope you've stopped trying. How about your boss's behavior? Your best friend's behavior? Your next-door neighbor's behavior? No, no, and no. Your children can do whatever they want. Whatever they choose. Your job is to teach your children control of their own behavior by applying rewards and consequences after their chosen behavior. I'm going to show you how to do this.

Focus on Behavior, Not Attitude

Studies have shown that 99.9 percent of children from 0 to 21 years of age have rotten attitudes. They are, to be politically correct, attitude-challenged. Every now and then you come across a kid with a genuinely good attitude. A real sweetheart. It's like a white rhino—it's extremely rare. Parents, you're going to have to put up with:

- the curled lip;
- the pouting;
- the whining;
- the sarcasm;
- the body language;
- the mean looks.

Kids can communicate so much with just a look, can't they? "I hate you!" "You're so stupid." "Life has passed you by, old-timer." "I could care less." You don't let disrespect, profanity, or insults pass without responding. There must be consequences for them. But you need to allow the basic, garden-variety bad attitude. It's impossible to get rid of a bad attitude, short of brain surgery. That's messy, expensive, and your insurance won't cover it. It is possible to help them improve their behavior. And that's just what my discipline strategy will help you do.

A Strategy for War

You need a strategy because if you wing it in discipline, you'll get run over repeatedly by your kids. You'll have tire tracks and sneaker prints all over your back. You're in a war, my friends—

a nasty, guerrilla war. You have to be smart, on your toes, because you're up against a worthy opponent. Children are clever and committed to their cause. They want fun and freedom, and you're in the way. Kids lie awake at night figuring out how to outwit you. They have the energy and the free time. You do not. Speaking for myself, at night I sleep the sleep of the exhausted. You can win the war, but only when you have a strategy, a battle plan. I have one for you.

Here is my general strategy: You create a reasonable set of behavior standards and apply reasonable rewards or consequences based on your children's behavior. It's a behavior-based system. The message you send to your children is this:

You are free to live as you choose. It is important that you learn how to live responsibly. So we (or I, if you're a single parent) have developed a reasonable set of behavior standards. If you meet these standards, you will be rewarded. If you choose not to, you will face the consequences.

All kids want independence. They're always saying, "I want to do things my way!" With my system, you say, "Go ahead. Do things your way. But based on your choices, there will be rewards or consequences." My system is God's system. When we obey His standards in the Bible, He rewards us. When we don't, He applies consequences. He is acting out of love, with our good in mind, as we should.

The goal of this strategy is making the focus the behavior of your children and the rewards or consequences that they earn. They choose to be rewarded or choose to earn consequences. It's up to them! Keep in mind, you cannot control your children's behavior. But you do control, rigidly, the rewards and consequences you apply. You must apply rewards and consequences each time, consistently, or the whole system collapses. Remember: Consistency is as strategic as the rewards and consequences.

I'm going to lead you through a specific four-step strategy. If you're married, work as a team. That's God's Plan A. If you are a single parent or your spouse refuses to be involved, do it yourself with the support of family, friends, church, and by praying and trusting God for the courage and strength. This is Plan B, but with God's help, it will be just as effective as Plan A. Let's cover the first two steps.

Establish Reasonable Standards of Behavior

You need to cover all the major areas: grades, chores, curfew, respect, moral/spiritual areas, social life, driving, and church life. In developing your list of standards, you must talk with a number of interested parties. Talk with your children. Ask them what standards they feel would be reasonable. If you involve your kids, chances are better they'll buy into the plan. Most importantly, talk with your spouse, who is your team member and co-leader. Talk to other parents—your peers as well as older parents who have done an excellent job raising their kids. Tap into their wisdom and experience! Talk to church leaders—Sunday school teachers, lay leaders, and the pastors. Talk with your support system of family and friends.

Your standards will depend on what kind of kid you've got. You look at age, personality, abilities, strengths, and weaknesses. You'll have slightly different standards for each of your children, because they're different from one another. Your kids, like all kids, will whine, "It's not fair!" Don't even go there. Your response is brief and to the point: "It's not about fairness. It's about differences."

Know each child so your standards will be attainable, not

too high or too low. For example, don't require straight A's from a C student. Not all kids are gifted academically. Do some research and be able to say, "I expect an A in English, a C in math, a B in history, and a B in science." Don't force piano lessons on a kid who just isn't musical. That's not a reasonable standard. Find another activity that the child enjoys.

Be specific so your children know exactly what you expect. "Do your best" sounds nice, and it is a good, basic principle, but it doesn't go far enough. Tell them what you think is their best. And use behavioral measures. Let me explain. Don't say, "You need to pull your weight around this house, Bobby." What does that mean? Nobody, including Bobby, knows. Tell Bobby exactly what chores he is to do and the time frame. Don't say, "We expect good grades, Susan. Good, solid grades. Is that clear, young lady?" Actually, no. It's not clear. You ought to say, "We expect at least all B's, Susan, and a C in geometry." That's clear.

Establish Reasonable Rewards and Consequences

The heart of my battle plan is the rewards and consequences your children earn with their behavior. As you develop your list of rewards and consequences, round up and talk to the usual suspects (the same persons you went to in drawing up your behavior standards): spouse, other parents, friends. . . . Again, you want to be reasonable. Your consequences should not be too harsh or too lenient. Your rewards should not be too extravagant or too paltry. For each major standard of behavior, you attach a reward and a consequence.

In the next several chapters, I'll provide you with the consequences and rewards I have found most effective in maintaining the discipline of children of all ages.

SIXTEEN

Paying the Piper:
Consequences for Younger Kids

"It's Not My Fault!"

While she was pregnant, a Seattle woman drank up to half a fifth of bourbon a day. As a result, her son was born retarded and malformed. She sued the makers of the bourbon for not warning her that she was harming her unborn child.

A woman smoked heavily her entire adult life. She had part of a cancerous lung removed and yet continued to smoke. Her doctors told her if she didn't stop smoking, she'd be dead inside of two years. She kept right on smoking. Inside of two years, she died of cancer. End of story, right? Wrong. Her relatives sued the tobacco company for causing her death.

A man planned a boating trip for the coming weekend. He watched a local twenty-four-hour weather channel to check the conditions. The weather forecast was for smooth seas and clear skies. But while he was on the water, a quick-moving storm came up and the high waves sank his boat. It was a total loss. He was rescued, but he wasn't as grateful as he was angry. He sued the weather channel for not warning him about the storm.

And here's my personal favorite. A young man strapped a refrigerator to his back and walked the course of a local footrace. No one made him do it. It was his own idea. After suffering severe injuries to his back (duh!), he sued the makers of the refrigerator. He said the company had failed to warn him of the potential consequences of carrying their product on his back.

I wish I could say these stories are isolated, ridiculous exceptions to the rule. But I can't. All over the world, people are filing lawsuits to take revenge (and get money) for accidents or foolish actions they took! No one seems to be willing to take the blame for choices anymore. There is an entire class of people, millions strong, who want to make others pay for their mistakes. My theory is, these individuals had parents who didn't have the courage to apply consequences. When children don't suffer proper punishment for their poor choices, they grow up to be professional victims and blamers.

Do not let this happen to your kids! Kids, by nature, want to avoid paying the price for their bad behavior. They'll lie, cheat, and distort the truth in a desperate attempt to escape consequences. How many times have you asked your kids who committed a particular offense (wrote on the wall, clogged the toilet, called Tokyo on the phone), only to have each one of them say with a straight face, "Not me." You could show your kid a videotape of him calling Tokyo, and he'd still deny it and try to worm out of the punishment. Because you love your children and want them to become honest, responsible adults, you must apply consequences after disobedient behavior.

Truth and Consequences

You can use just about anything to punish your children. I want you to feel free, with a few exceptions. Food, water, and shelter are off-limits. I know it can be tempting, but don't use these. You wouldn't say, "Bobby, you're sleeping in the front yard tonight." Also, don't use church time. It's okay to keep them from going to a special youth activity, but not regular, in-church programs. You don't want to hold them back from worshiping God and learning more about Him. Also, I don't recommend withholding individual one-on-one time with a parent as a consequence. This is relationship-building time, and I wouldn't tamper with it.

Spankers of the World, Unite!

Spanking is effective punishment for children who are, roughly, fifteen months to six or seven years old. (It is not for teenagers. Spanking teenagers is humiliating and counterproductive.) My life verse as a parent is Proverbs 22:15: "Folly is bound up in the heart of a child, but the rod of discipline will drive it far from him." Yes! I read that verse and cheer! God says spanking is a valuable tool in discipline, and He hasn't changed His mind.

Spanking is for defiance and willful disobedience. When your child shakes his fist in your face and says, "No, I won't do it!" that's a spanking offense. You'll say, "I will now apply Proverbs 22:15 to your backside." He'll ask, "What's Proverbs 22:15?" You'll reply, as you begin the spanking, "Read your Bible, son."

Spanking is also for protection from danger. The only way I taught little William Clarke not to go into the road in front of our home was spanking. It's a busy road and cars zip by. After the fourth or fifth spanking, William learned it didn't pay to go into the road. If I'd tried to reason with him, he'd be dead now. You can't reason with small kids! They don't know what you're talking about. Don't waste your breath. Spank, and they'll get the message.

The pain of spanking helps break the will. Not the spirit, but the will. You have to break the will of every child—and the sooner, the better. There's nothing quite as ugly, or dangerous, as a teenager or young adult with an unbroken will. If you don't break a child's will, she'll break you.

Spanking is done privately. It's not a spectator sport. You don't say, "Gather around, kids. I'm going to spank Susie!" And you are angry when you spank. I get a kick out of the experts who say, "Never spank a child in anger." Well, of course you're angry! You don't spank when you're in a good mood, do you? "Come here, Susie. Mom's happy, and so I think I'll spank you." You're angry, but not in a rage. Sometimes, we all get too angry. When that happens, back off and cool down. You'll still be angry but in control.

Three to five swats are usually enough. Don't spank until the kid cries or begs for mercy. Use your hand or some kind of a paddle. Spank the bottom only. And never should a child ever be struck in any way, on any other part of the body. Leave the child alone, then return to talk. You want an apology. A real apology—to you, to anyone else the child offended, and to God. You make it clear that disobedience is not just against you but also against God. A real apology shows a broken will, which is exactly what you want. When the apology is offered, give the child affection. The relationship goes back to normal. If there is no apology, don't spank again. Move right into time-out.

After one of my parenting seminars, one parent told me that she requires a written apology after particularly mean behavior. The child writes out an apology to the parent, any other person involved, and God. Also, the child must include appropriate Scripture that bears on his disobedient act. Then, the child reads the apology out loud to the family. I like that idea. It might be helpful if you're dealing with a strong-willed kid.

If done correctly, spanking will not teach your children to hit others. That it will is a common liberal view, and it's not true. Now, if you physically abuse your children (hit, punch, kick), that will certainly cause emotional damage and lead to them hitting others. But if you spank in the controlled way I've described—God's way—then it teaches self-control and obedience.

Time-Out for Acting Out

Time-out is sending your young child (or taking him kicking and screaming, as the case may be) to an environment devoid of any entertainment or pleasure for a period of time. Time-out is typically used for behavior short of outright defiance. Use a bathroom. The kid's room is too much fun and way too comfortable. In his room, the kid has all his special things: bed, toys, special blanket, music, etc. There's nothing to do in a bathroom except go to the bathroom. After that, the kid is just sitting on the pot. Reverse the lock if necessary, to keep the kid inside. Some ornery kids will just come waltzing right out.

Ten to fifteen minutes is a good rule of thumb. If the kid screams or makes a racket after ten minutes, time is added. "For each minute you scream, I'll double the time you spend in there." The kid could be in there for a while, but you hold the line. If he has to use the bathroom, no problem. He's already there. If he gets thirsty, there's plenty of water in there. "Drink out of the toilet, honey. It doesn't hurt the dog." Food isn't a problem. Just give him food that slips under the door: hot dogs, bread, potato chips. If he's made a mess, he must clean it up before he comes out.

When the time is up, go to the child and talk. Again, as with spanking, you want an apology. No apology, no release from jail. A strong-willed child will refuse to apologize. Fine. When it's bedtime, he'll go from time-out in the bathroom to his room. There will also be serious consequences the next day: more time-out, loss of the use of toys, no videos or television, no playing outside, etc.

A real tough, strong-willed child will not give you the reaction you want. The will of a strong-willed kid is a lot tougher to break than the will of the typical, normal child. Don't expect, or try to get, a penitent reaction. He—or she—won't give you the satisfaction of showing you true brokenness. "Spank me more—you're not hurting me." Or, "I'll sit in this bathroom all week, and you'll never get me to apologize!" Just stay the course and continue to use spanking and time-out. Show no reaction. Eventually, brokenness will take place inside. This kind of kid won't admit any change of heart, but you'll see proof of a broken will in improved behavior.

You spank or use time-out as soon as possible after the misbehavior. This clearly connects the misbehavior to the consequence. The same principle applies to rewards. If you catch your child being good, reward her right away. If the reward isn't soon, small kids will forget what it's for.

Spanking and time-out are effective for younger children because they really have no life. What do you take away from a kid who has nothing? All younger kids do is eat, sleep, go the bathroom, and bother you! Older kids have more in their lives and you can take what they have, piece by piece. (More on this in the next chapter.)

Shunning Isn't Just for the Amish

Another effective corrective measure is a technique called extinguishing. (No, it has nothing to do with spraying your kid with a fire extinguisher.) This is a fancy name for ignoring behavior you don't like. It's particularly effective for fits, whining, when a kid asks over and over for something, and when a kid goes into that one special mode that drives you insane. He is hateful, angry, hostile, verbally abusive, or all of the above. A kid acts in these ways to get what he wants and to get a reaction from you. And he'll settle for either one.

When your kid moves into that mode, you ignore him. You don't respond. You say nothing. You have no reaction. You go about your business as if nothing is happening. You continue your conversation with your spouse, keep watching television, doing the laundry, reading your book, or cooking the evening meal. Life moves on, but the kid simply doesn't exist. He has become invisible. It's just like the Amish and their shunning a member of the community who has broken an important rule. When the kid stops the behavior, he becomes visible again; things go back to normal. You give attention. You talk to him. You act as though nothing happened. It's like time stood still. Of course, he doesn't get what he wanted.

Extinguishing serves two purposes. One, it can modify your child's behavior. With no reinforcement of any kind, the kid will eventually stop the behavior. Second, it prevents you from doing or saying anything you'll regret. If you respond to the kid's annoying mode, it's easy to overreact. To blow up. To say things that hurt your child.

The Bedtime Blues

Bedtime with small children can be one of the most frustrating times of the day. It is a very difficult area for many parents, so don't feel too badly. You've got a lot of company. I see many couples and single parents who allow their evenings to be ruined by a kid who won't go to bed. You need to succeed in this area because you need a break. You need several hours for yourself and your marriage. "My day with you is over," are words you must say and enforce.

I've got good news. Unless your child has some specific sleep disorder, you can get the job done. You can end a kid's day and have some time for your life. You don't have much of a life when you have kids, but you're entitled to something. The bottom line is this: Get tough and stop reinforcing the anti-bedtime behavior.

One parent is usually the wimp. That's the parent the kid targets. I'm talking to you wimps. Stop rocking the child. Stop singing, even if you have the voice of a diva. Stop lying down in bed with the kid. Stop running to the child when she cries for you. You are reinforcing the behavior of not going to sleep. You'd cry too, if you could get Mommy and Daddy to come in and coddle you. Such elaborate, lengthy bedtime behaviors don't work! When you eventually leave, the kid still screams her head off. Your kid has to learn how to put herself to sleep. It's a basic life skill. Do you want to still be doing it for her when she's seventeen? Thirty-five?

If you're married, work together. Especially when you're beginning this new program, do it as a team. A show of unity and force lets the kid know you mean business. If you're single, don't worry. You can still do the job.

Establish the same bedtime every night. Consistency helps. Use the same routine in the half hour leading up to bedtime. We have our last drink, we read a story, we brush our little toofies, we put on our pj's, etc. No snacks or drinks just before bed. We don't want a sugar rush. We don't want more energy. We don't want them to pee (or worse), do we? We don't want their little bladders full, do we? No, we don't.

Eliminate rowdy games and wild roughhousing just before bed. Dads are usually the guilty ones here. Put the child in the room and in bed. You can spend a few minutes (five to ten, maximum) to talk, to unwind, to tuck in, and to pray. Then, you leave. . .and you stay gone. If he cries, let him cry. Crying won't hurt him. It's good for him. It cleans out his lungs. It helps tire him out, so he can sleep. Crying is a beautiful thing.

Be prepared for some serious crying. Oh, the pitiful cries you're going to hear! There's nothing quite like the wretched wailing of the truly desperate child. Turn on the television or radio to block the sounds. Let at least twenty minutes go by before you go to the child, briefly, and say one comforting but firm sentence ("Suck it up, Sammy"). Then leave again. If you're married, go together. The secret is to act like you don't care. You pretend it's not fazing you. This tough exterior will crush his hopes of sucking you in. Your child may say, accusingly, "You don't even care!" Your response, with a hint of a smile, is, "You're right. I don't."

If the kid has the gall to leave his room, lock him in. Sandy and I have locked all our sleep-challenged kids in their rooms at one time or another. Simply reverse the locks. Leave a nightlight on. After he has dropped off, unlock and open the door.

If the kid cries during the night, after you're in bed, it's the same drill. Go and deal with him briefly (together, if you are married), then leave. If he comes to your bed, quickly escort him back to his bed. Do not let a child sleep in your bed, unless he's sick or genuinely terrified of something. Even in that case, it's better to take him to his bed and lie down with him. The message is: You sleep in your bed, not mine (or ours). If you allow the child to sleep in your bed, you'll be stuck with the world's biggest fidget. Most kids thrash around in their sleep. Plus, and this is the critical part, you will establish a pattern. He'll like it in your bed and keep coming. You need your undisturbed sleep. You and your spouse need the time alone. And then, there's your child's full bladder to think of. . . .

SEVENTEEN

Taking Pieces of a Life: Consequences for Older Kids

"I'm Not As Dumb As You Think"

When children hit eleven years of age, they go through an amazing transformation. It's a drastic, dramatic change that turns a family upside down. Suddenly, and without warning, eleven-year-old children become brilliant. Overnight, they gain wisdom and insight beyond their years. They go to bed regular kids and wake up Albert Einsteins. They know how the world works. They have a firm command of the truth in every field of study. They understand the mysteries of life. They speak with authority on issues they haven't studied. Eleven year olds don't have to study and gain knowledge with time and hard work. That process is only for run-of-the-mill, average drones. Eleven year olds can build a mountain of theory from one tiny shred of information they overheard in the school hallway. They don't have to research the topic. What a waste of time that would be! They just know. They just know everything.

Their arguments are often ridiculous and make no sense at all, but they expect the Nobel Prize for their insights. If we try to correct them and point out the flaw in their reasoning, they shake their heads sadly in amusement. They pity us because our aging brains can no longer keep up with them. You see, as their brains expand and swell, our brains contract and shrivel. The eleven year olds of this world really believe parents are a

164

bunch of doddering old fools who don't have a clue. We can't possibly match their superior intellectual prowess. And, unfortunately for us parents, this phenomenon just gets worse in the years to come. The older kids get, the smarter they think they are, and the dumber they think we are. They think we're idiots! They can't believe we've lived so long and yet know so little. To them, parents are outdated relics of the past who can't hope to outwit them. Ah, the arrogance of youth!

What our kids don't realize is that we're not as dumb as they think we are. We are getting older and somewhat creakier, but we haven't lost it yet. As a matter of fact, we know more than they do. A lot more. We can outsmart them. We can stay one jump ahead of them. We can teach them what they must know about life without them even knowing we're doing it. One of the ways we teach life skills is through consequences. We will, over and over again, correct bad behavior by hitting them where it hurts. Through the pain of consequences will come critical tools for living a successful life.

You Name It, You Can Use It

You can use anything older kids value for punishment. The list goes on and on: television, video and computer games, computer time, compact disc player, music tapes, telephone time, car, job, bicycle, skateboard, bedtime, money. . . . All kids have certain things they like. That's what you take—piece by little piece. Withholding junk food, snacks, and dessert are excellent consequences. "Hey, where are the Twinkies, the Pepsi, and the potato chips?" "They're gone, Bobby. Because of your behavior, there will be no snacks for three days. But help yourself to the cauliflower and carrot sticks." Keep feeding them the basic meals, of course: "Here are your vegetables. Eat up, honey." The nice thing about this consequence is there are more snacks available for you.

School activities and sports are fair game. If your kid is in an extracurricular activity or sport, you can take it away. She misses a practice or a game. Some parents tell me, "But that hurts the whole team!" I say, "Yes, it does. And whose fault is that?" The parents mumble, "Well, I guess it's Susie's fault." I reply, "Yeah, I guess it is." Always have the kid call the coach or the leader of the activity and explain why she can't be there. Listen in so her explanation is accurate, and that she is actually talking to the person. She might get a little inventive: "Coach, my mom's a real witch! I think she's manic-depressive!" You say to your child, "If baseball is important to you, I guess you'll follow our rules."

Kids cherish their free time, so it is a valuable tool to use against them. After poor behavior, you reduce free time—each day and on the weekends. You confine them to the house. It's house arrest. Each day, your kid is responsible to do chores, homework, and other behavior you specify. If he fails to carry out his responsibilities, then he doesn't do anything fun that day and must stay inside.

I also recommend a weekly system. Each Friday, there is a brief meeting with the child to evaluate her grades and behavior for that week. You give your evaluation of her home behavior, and the child's teachers give their school evaluations. Each Friday, your child takes an evaluation sheet to each of her teachers. Each teacher makes comments on grades and behavior and signs the sheet. If your child fails to get input from all her teachers ("Oh, I wonder why he missed Miss Ratchet, the math teacher?"), the hammer falls. This weekly evaluation determines the weekend your child will have, as well as the whole next week. Every Friday, she has a brand-new chance to avoid consequences and earn rewards. School is a kid's number one job. Don't wait nine weeks for their grades! Kids are always surprised by poor grades. If there are poor grades at the end of a week, you say, "I guess you need more time to study. So, I will give you more time."

If you really want to cause pain and anguish, (and change behavior), limit the kid's social life. Going to a friend's house, hanging out at the mall, and attending parties are all on the table. Dating can also be suspended. Dating isn't a right. It's not mentioned in the United States Constitution. "You will not talk on the phone or go out with Bubba for one week." Your daughter will whine, "I can't live without seeing Bubba for a week!" "Then I guess we'll plan a funeral, because you ain't seeing him." And you'll add, "If Bubba means so much to you, then I guess you'll follow the rules."

Natural and Logical Consequences

Natural consequences are the consequences that naturally occur following a behavior. It's simply allowing nature to run its course. You, the parent, do nothing. God is the One who came up with the idea of natural consequences: "A man reaps what he sows" (Galatians 6:7). If your kid works hard in school, he will get good grades. If he goofs off, he'll get poor grades. If your daughter breaks driving laws, she'll get a ticket and may end up in an accident. If your son lies to his friends, they won't trust him.

Don't step in to save your child from natural consequences. There are some lessons that only life can teach. I know parents who have marched in to complain to a teacher about a low grade. The kid earned the low grade, but Mommy and Daddy tried to get it raised. Once I saw a couple in therapy whose son got busted for dealing drugs. They admitted to me he was guilty of the crime. I told these Christian parents to have their son plead guilty and throw himself on the mercy of the court. They disagreed and ended up mortgaging their home to pay for an expensive attorney. Their son pled not guilty! It was disgraceful.

You intervene only in a situation when serious physical harm or injustice will take place. If William goes into the road, I won't let him get hit by a car. I'll run out there and save him. Then, I'll spank his bottom. If others are lying, and your kid is being blamed for something he didn't do, you will take action. But if your kid made a poor choice, let life's natural consequences follow.

Logical consequences are the consequences you as the parent apply. There are many times, like with poor grades, you will apply logical consequences on top of natural consequences. Try to make sure the consequences are logically related to the misbehavior. If you can connect the two logically, the consequence has more punch and will be remembered. There's a better chance change will be created. In other words, the punishment should fit the crime.

The wrong approach would be: The kid fails to take out the trash, and you ground him for one week. Where's the logical connection? Here's the right way: The kid fails to take out the trash, and you make him eat part of the trash. I'm kidding, of course. A logical consequence would be not paying him for that job.

Here are more examples. The kid breaks a curfew; he's grounded for one week. You see, that's logical: He was out late, so he doesn't go out again for a while. The kid drives poorly or misuses the car; his or her driving privileges are suspended for a period of time. The kid misuses the television; no television for a period of time. The kids abuses his telephone privileges; no phone. The kid makes a mess; she cleans it up. The kid fails to put dirty clothes in the hamper; you don't wash them. Your kid will complain, "But my clothes smell! I have nothing clean to wear to school." You say, "Don't worry, son, I think most of the other kids smell, too." I'll just bet you'll find your son's clothes in the hamper later on that day.

Make Consequences Specific and Time-Limited

Consequences need to be specific so they're clear. They need to be time-limited to provide consistency and hope. Don't say, "You're grounded for life!" It's kind of impossible to enforce this consequence. "I'm twenty-four now, Dad. Can I go out now?" "No. I said for life, Bobby!"

It's better to clearly define the grounding. "You are grounded for one week, beginning tonight and going through next Monday night. Grounded means no telephone calls to or from friends, no dates, no friends over, no visits to friends' houses, and no use of the car except to and from school. Each violation of the grounding rules will add one day to the grounding." Theoretically, it could be for life, but that's unlikely. Have the kid repeat the consequences so you can know she has it. Close all the loopholes. All kids are born lawyers.

For major violations, your consequences will be more severe, last longer, and remain in place until real change occurs. I had a case where an eighteen-year-old boy showed disrespect for his dad big-time in front of the entire family. I recommended the dad lower the boom. The boy's car was taken away for a minimum of two weeks. He had to apologize to the entire family—and mean it. He had to show real, measurable change in a number of areas before the car was returned. There was an evaluation at the end of each week. As I recall, it took that boy four weeks to get his car back.

Creative Consequences

Be creative with some of your consequences. Come up with crazy, zany ideas to work at correcting your kids. The element of humor eases the blow and can help motivate change. This approach keeps your kids guessing and makes parenting more fun for you. For example, I saw a mom in therapy who came up with an ingenious way to get her kids up in the morning. She was having fits dragging them out of bed in time to leave for school. They were chronically late and ruined her mornings. She decided to take action. Her plan was to give them one wake-up call at 6:45 A.M. If they weren't up by 7:00, she'd walk in and soak them with a pitcher of ice water—right in the kisser. She told me that after a few soakings, they became early risers. The kids could hear the ice machine and the splashing of the water in the pitcher as Mom came down the hallway. You never saw kids leap so fast out of bed.

Another mom used funny, silly behaviors as consequences for her son. Her behavior wasn't mean. Just tongue-in-cheek. Her method was to make him do more of the unacceptable, impulsive, immature actions he engaged in at home. If he ran in the house, she'd say, "Okay, everybody outside and let's watch Jimmy (not his real name) run." The whole family, and neighborhood kids, too, if they were present, would troop outside.

She had Jimmy run laps and wind sprints. If Jimmy (who was an aggressive child) pushed someone else, she'd say, "I guess you like to push. So let's do some pushing." She'd make him push the wall for a few minutes. There was a time when Jimmy had a bad habit of spitting. That's right—you guessed it—when she caught him spitting, she'd say, "I guess you like to spit. Here's a bucket. Fill it up."

Don't Nag, Just Get Even

At most, only ask your child one time to do something. Tell her exactly what you want done, and give a time frame: right now, within ten minutes, by 5:00 P.M. If the job isn't done correctly or within the time frame, lay a consequence on the kid. She'll still do the job but then suffer the consequence. This approach will save you a lot of time, energy, and stress. It will also improve your relationship with your child.

When you keep reminding a kid to do something, you are a nag. You get angrier and angrier, don't you? Finally, you lose it. "Cindy, I've told you to pick up your clothes five times! Pick them up, now!" Actually it's your own mistake for telling her five times. That's four times too many. When you lose it, it's your fault in the kid's mind. You are the issue, not the fact that she stalled and disobeyed and didn't do what you asked, when you asked.

Your kid wants you to lose it. She feels powerful: "Look what I did to Mom. She's freaking out!" A real difficult, strong-willed kid loves to get a reaction out of you. And this kind of kid is good at it. Your reaction is her payoff. She doesn't even care if you punish her. She got want she wanted. She got you mad.

When your child disobeys, you have to act as though you

don't care. You have to take all the emotion out of the situation. What the kid did means nothing to you. She acted out or did not do that chore—so what? You don't care. You point it out in an even, calm tone, and lay the consequences on her. "You made a poor choice, and here's the consequence." No anger. No hurt. No nagging. No emotional outbursts. No lectures.

If you can reduce the emotion and just hit the kid with the consequence, some nice things happen. First, you'll be in control, and you'll maintain your dignity and respect. When you lose it, you really do look stupid: distorted facial features like bulging eyes, neck veins swelling, and flecks of foam spraying from your mouth. Second, there's no payoff for the kid. There's no attention and no power. Just the consequence. Maybe—just maybe—the kid will walk away blaming herself. Third, you don't waste your precious time nagging, blowing up, and then having to apologize. The kid makes a mistake, you lower the boom with surgical precision, and life moves on. My mother has a saying: "The little dogs bark, but the caravan moves on."

Make Misbehavior a Family Issue

The power and support of the family is often overlooked in the process of discipline. The family is God's designed unit to help us learn, grow, and adjust in life (Deuteronomy 6:5–7). Let's use it!

When a child misbehaves, at first you deal only with that child. If the child is genuinely repentant and demonstrates change, you can keep the matter confidential. The rest of the family will know generally what's going on, but you keep the details private.

But if there is no repentance and no change, take it to the

family. If your child has an unhealthy, serious behavior pattern that is not improving—alcohol, drugs, sex, cheating in school, poor grades, lying, disrespect for parents and authority figures, breaking the law, associating with bad peers—take it to the family. If your child is directly harming another family member—vicious sibling rivalry, verbal abuse, stealing—take it to the family. If a child is adversely affecting the harmony of the family, take it to the family. Take it to the family means you call a meeting of the immediate nuclear family. Everyone living under one roof attends the meeting. If Grandma is in the back bedroom, drag her to the meeting. . .well, just ask her to come. The misbehaving child is at the meeting, even if you have to hold her down.

You reveal the specific problem in detail. First, you ask the child to tell the family about the problem. If she refuses, then you do it, perhaps explaining that it might be fairer and more accurate if she explained things in her own words. You go over all of it, chapter and verse. The consequence of the whole family knowing carries some weight. Even a hard-nosed kid will feel the heat. Since one member's behavior affects the whole family, the family has a right to know. Plus, a family is supposed to be a group whose members love each other and care about one another.

In this initial meeting, the parent in charge asks each member to comment on the situation. You go around the room and, one by one, everyone shares, following just a few simple rules (for example, no insults allowed, no self-righteousness). Family members can express anger, hurt, and disappointment. Members can admit how they've contributed to the problem. Plans and strategies for solving the problem can be discussed. Members can share how they handled a similar problem in their lives.

The support, feedback, and advice of the family is invaluable in solving the problem. It's the family working together to help one of its own. It's not an individual problem. It's a family problem. The family members don't trash the misbehaving child; they try to help. When one family member hurts, everybody hurts. Like the church, when one member rejoices, the others rejoice with her; when one member suffers, the others suffer, too (1 Corinthians 12:26).

What I am suggesting is similar to what I do as a psychologist in family therapy. I bring the whole family together in my office. I never know who will be the key to change. Sometimes it's the youngest member. Sometimes it's the oldest. I've seen God use family meetings time and time again to create real healing and change.

At the end of this meeting, the family prays for the acting-out child and the family. Each member offers a prayer. It's vital to involve God and ask for His help. Jesus gave us two wonderful promises in Matthew 18:19–20:

> *"Again, I tell you that if two of you on earth*
> *agree about anything you ask for,*
> *it will be done for you by my Father in heaven.*
> *For where two or three*
> *come together in my name,*
> *there am I with them."*

No problem is ever solved without God.

Have regular family meetings to check on the child's progress and to hold her accountable. You can use your regular once-a-week family meeting to deal with this ongoing situation. Difficult problems take time to fix, so a number of meetings may be necessary. Meet for as many weeks as it takes to achieve a breakthrough. After all, a member of the family is worth the trouble.

You might want to try a technique I often use with my families in therapy. I ask the parents to each write a letter to the misbehaving child. The letter consists of two parts. One, all the resentments they feel for the child. Two, what they admit is their responsibility for the problem. They confess their personal failings and shortcomings as parents. I ask the child to write the same letter: her resentment against her parents and her responsibility in creating and maintaining the problem. Then, I have all three read their letters out loud in front of the entire family in a session. It's powerful, and it can be very healing. I make it clear when I give the assignment that it has three goals: to get all the issues out on the table, to begin to clean out all resentments and promote forgiveness, and to begin a process of change. After the letters are read, they are burned with the whole family watching.

In certain situations, it's a good idea to add others outside the nuclear family to your meetings: extended family, close family friends, teachers, coaches, pastors, etc. If the one-on-one approach doesn't work, you go to the nuclear family meetings. If the nuclear family meetings don't work, call in more troops. You may have to end up renting a gymnasium. Matthew chapter 18 teaches us this very principle. When someone is in sin, go to him individually. If he doesn't listen, go to him with two or three others. If he still won't listen, go to the church body with the problem. So if your child doesn't respond, keep adding more persons to the process.

EIGHTEEN

Obedience Has Its Rewards

Nightmare on Main Street

S everal years ago, the five of us (William wasn't around yet) drove to Orlando to spend the day at Disney World. We hadn't been there for a while, and Sandy and I thought the kids would really enjoy it. As I paid several hundred dollars for our entrance tickets, it began to dawn on me why we hadn't been there for a while. That day was the longest day of my life. It still gives me the willies to think about it.

It was hot. Brutally hot. The heat was not just from the sun. It was body heat coming from the unbelievable mass of humanity clogging every square foot of the Magic Kingdom. We waited in interminable lines for everything. We waited to see Mickey and Minnie. We waited to get a drink of water. We waited for the little train that chugs around the park. We waited to order lunch. We waited until a table opened up for lunch. (I had to yell, "Fire!" to clear some space.) We waited to throw out our trash from lunch. We waited to go the bathrooms. But most of all, we waited in line for the rides. Hours and hours of waiting for rides, each of which lasted a couple of minutes.

My breaking point came at the Dumbo ride late in the afternoon. Leeann just had to go on Dumbo, so we joined the back of the line. You couldn't even see the ride from where we were. I really thought I was going to die in that line.

Several folks ahead of us did collapse from heatstroke, and I silently cheered when their absence moved the line a few yards. Hey, it was survival of the fittest. After an hour and a half, we finally got there and climbed in the Flying Dumbo vehicle. We rose up and flew in a circle for a lousy, crummy, and insulting ninety seconds. As Dumbo returned to earth, I told Leeann to stay put. When the uniformed attendant came up to ask us to get out, I said through clenched teeth, "I waited an hour and a half for this pitiful ninety seconds. We're going around again." I think that scene cost us the chance to be the featured family in the next Main Street Parade. I didn't actually have the nerve to stay on the ride. I realized I would have been torn to bits by the poor suckers still waiting for their ninety-second ride.

Leeann and I left the scene of the Dumbo nightmare and met up with Sandy and the other two girls at a predetermined spot. One look at Sandy and I knew her day had been even worse than mine. Nancy had thrown up all over the front of Mom's dress. Not spit up. Thrown up. Upchucked. You could smell her thirty yards away. That was the second thing that disqualified us from being the parade family. Sandy told me later that a lady had asked her, "Did you know your child threw up all over you?" Sandy told her, "No! Really? Is that what this awful-smelling stuff is all over my dress?" There were two good results from Nancy's little accident. One, it certainly cleared a path through the crowd. Two, it brought our day to an end. Sandy said to me, "We're going home." I didn't argue.

The five of us came dragging down Main Street. Sandy and I were exhausted and in extremely foul moods. If Goofy had gotten in my way, I would have flattened him. It should have been obvious to everyone that we needed to go home. But what did my two older daughters do? Did Emily and Leeann thank us for the day? Did they sympathize with our ragged, limp-as-a-noodle condition? Did they, at the least, have the common courtesy to be quiet? No. Guess what they did. They cried and whined and begged to go on just a few more rides. They told us we couldn't leave Disney World early! They said we just had to stay for them. They wanted more fun and we owed it to them. If you want to know what happened when we got back to the car, read my section on spanking in chapter 16.

This story doesn't surprise any of you, does it? I'm sure you could tell many stories just like it. All kids believe that their parents owe them a very nice living. They take and take and take and come back for more. They have an inborn, ingrained entitlement attitude. Kids also believe they shouldn't have to do anything in return for all the wonderful pleasures afforded them in life. They fully expect their parents to grant their every whim just because these darlings are alive. Their motto is, "We didn't ask to be born. But now that we're here, you've got to give us what we want."

Everything Is a Reward

Part of good parenting is correcting this entitlement attitude. In fact, there are only a few physical things kids are entitled to: food, water, shelter, clothing, and medical care. That's it. Everything—and I mean everything—else is a luxury item and, therefore, a reward. Rewards are the same things you take away to create consequences. It is the same list I used in chapter 17. Basically, rewards are anything your kids value. You put the whole enchilada, whatever they like, on the table.

The trick is to find out what each kid values. Then, you can use the rewards to motivate. Some parents ask me, "Why do we have to use rewards? Shouldn't kids just do things because those things are right? Surely you're not telling me we should reward children for being good?" My reply is, "Get real. Join me in the real world!" You have to motivate kids. Eventually, they'll internalize and do good things because it makes them feel good inside and because it will please God. But this process takes time! God uses rewards. He always has. When we obey His standards, He rewards us. There will be rewards in heaven (Luke 6:23).

Ask your kid what he wants in return for a behavior you want him to do. Cut a deal! If he's an older kid, does he want money, television time, phone time, computer time, or a later bedtime? If he's a younger kid, does he want a special video, to play with a special toy, to play outside, or a coloring book or stickers?

Sandy's potty training method was simple and effective. And based on rewards. If the child went to the pot, she got a chocolate treat. If she wet her pants, she got nothing. And she had to clean up her mess. That was the consequence part. Wiping up a yellow river, or picking up a Number Two and putting it in the pot was not pleasant. Of course, we didn't make the kids use their bare hands. And the whole affair was not emotionally charged but matter-of-fact.

Let's say you want to motivate your child to read. If you're like Sandy and me, you consider reading of the utmost importance. You need to model reading. You need to read often to your kid. You need to find enjoyable books for him to read. And you need to cut a deal. In return for twenty minutes a day of reading, what does he want? It's not enough to say, "You know, Billy, reading is very important. So, we'd like you read more. Okay?" Initially, you motivate him to read with rewards.

When he eventually enjoys reading, his own enjoyment will be his reward.

Make Your Child Earn Rewards

All kids think the things they value are God-given rights, and they shouldn't have to do anything in return for them. Wrong! Your kids must earn rewards and keep on earning them. "The last time I checked, Bobby, you weren't part of the Royal Family. No, we're just common people, and we all have to work for what we get."

If you just hand out rewards regardless of children's behavior, you spoil them! They have no incentive to improve their behavior. You feed the entitlement attitude they already have by nature. You've got to teach your children that, in life, rewards are earned by hard work. It's true, they could eventually go on welfare and be supported by the government. But that won't be much of a life.

I worked with a dad whose teenage son had gotten hooked on drugs. He and his wife paid for several treatment programs, but the kid always went back to using. The dad came up with a plan he was sure would work. He decided to give his son a brand-new car. He told the boy, "If you stop using drugs and complete college, you can keep it." I told the dad he was crazy! This kid didn't deserve even a go-cart! The dad meant well, but his plan was a complete disaster. His son kept using drugs. You need to make a kid earn what he gets. If you give the reward first, you take away the motivation.

Whenever a child wants a reward, you ask, "What are you going to do to earn it?" If your son wants to watch a video, he will first put away his toys and help Mom dust. If your daughter wants to use the phone, she will have to first finish her homework and chores. If he wants to go outside and play, he'll get his chores done. If she wants dessert, she will eat a good dinner and help clean up after dinner. Now, you don't always do this. But almost always. Business before pleasure is a life principle kids need to learn before they leave your home.

Let's say your child wants a bigger reward: driving a car, going on a date, having you pay car insurance, or having a later curfew. Those are bigger privileges, and your child will have to produce bigger behavior to get them: grades high, chores done, behavior good, church attendance solid, and spiritual life strong.

I think you've got the picture. Everything is earned. My dad told me over and over, "David, if you decide to live a life-style we don't approve—drinking, drugs, sex, drifting from God —then we will not subsidize your lifestyle. We will not pay for private high school. We won't pay one thin dime for college. And you won't live here." This message helped keep me on the straight and narrow. To my parents, three things would determine whether or not my brother and I would receive rewards (including use of the car): our relationship with the Lord, our behavior, and our grades. This was a straight "reward/consequence" strategy.

Rewards Given Can Be Taken Away

Just because children have earned a reward doesn't mean they get to keep it. It all depends on their behavior. Kids think that once they earn a reward it's theirs, even if they blow it big-time behavior-wise. I say no. You can take back a reward if necessary.

Jimmy earns the right to watch a favorite video. Just before he puts it in the VCR, he starts a fight with his sister and slaps her across the face. What do you do? Easy. You yank the video, and you add some other consequences. He'll say, "But I earned that video!" You will say, "That's right, son, you did. But you just 'de-earned' it. But don't worry. You can earn it again, after you've paid this debt to society."

Susie earned your permission to go to her first formal banquet at school. It's a big deal! She has her dress, her date, and all the plans are in place. Susie's report card comes in a few days before the banquet, and it's a disaster: two F's, two D's, and one C. What do you do? You cancel the banquet. She knew she was doing poorly, and she said nothing to you. Some parents would say, "Oh, but what about her date? The poor guy's not going to be able to go now." Here's what I say to the young man: "Timmy, you rolled the dice when you asked my daughter out. You gambled, son. And, in this case, you lost! It's over!"

Losing the banquet is a bitter pill for Susie, but it'll be a consequence she'll never forget. "The parent giveth, and the parent taketh away" (Hezekiah 22:12). Okay, this verse isn't in the Bible. But the principle certainly is—all through both Testaments. Love is unconditional, but material gifts and rewards are not.

Even if your kid has bought something with his own money, you can take it away. The kid is living in your house, isn't he? Sometimes, you have to give your kid this message: "Me parent. You child. Me take." A single mom spoke to me at a parenting seminar I was presenting at her church. Her seventeen-year-old son had made a big mistake and she asked what consequence would be appropriate. I recommended, among other things, that she take away his car for a while. She said, "I can't do that. He bought his car, and he's paying his own car insurance." I said, "That doesn't make any difference. He lives in your home, doesn't he? You're the mom, aren't you? Take the car."

Cash Money Motivates

Go ahead and use money as a reward. It isn't the only reward you use, but it can be a powerful one. Use money in return for household chores. You pay a specific amount for a specific job. When it's done to your satisfaction and in your time frame, pay the kid. This is the way life works: Do a job; get paid. Isn't money one of the main reasons you work? Now, you don't give money for every single job. "Thanks for holding the door, John. Here's a fiver." Or, "I appreciate you helping carry the groceries in, Becky. Here's two dollars." I don't believe in tipping kids.

I like this system for chores: The kids are responsible for certain core chores. No money is given for these duties. They are done to help out the family to which they belong. If these regular chores aren't done, there are consequences. Then, there is also a list of extra jobs. For these, money is given. This system provides a good, realistic balance. In life, you're not paid for every job you do, especially around the house.

Money for good grades is a good idea. If it works for your kid, do it! Work out a deal: fifteen dollars for every A, ten dollars for a B, etc. I wouldn't pay for C's and D's. When you pay off, your kid will walk away and think, "Hah! What a sucker!" He'll laugh to himself as he counts his cash: "This is the easiest money I ever made." Well, the joke's on him. He studied, and he learned. That's all you care about.

Communicate the Plan

Remember my four-step battle plan? We have arrived at the third step: Communicate to your children the specific plan in each area. At this point, you have developed specific and easily understood behavior standards, rewards, and consequences. Attached to each behavior standard is a reward and a consequence. Put the main areas—the biggies—in writing to avoid confusion and to close loopholes. All parties sign the plan. It's a contract, something the children will deal with all their lives, beginning with buying a car and later, one of the most significant and sacred, the marriage contract. If it's verbal only, kids will "forget" the terms, or say, "You never said that." Post the original and keep several copies. It's amazing how these behavior contracts disappear.

It's a living contract and will be changed often. The child or parent can renegotiate. Of course, the child will have to convince you of the validity of the proposed changes. You have a different contract with each child. As changes occur, communicate them to your child. As each child gets older, or circumstances change, a renegotiation process is in order. You get input from the child, others in your circle of friends and advisors, and draw up a new plan with the changes. This whole plan also gives you, the parent, ample opportunity to stress, throughout the growing-up years of your children, that certain standards are not, and never will be, negotiable.

How to Apply Consequences

Step Four is: Apply the rewards and consequences. Applying rewards is easy. The child has done well, made a good choice, and everybody's happy. Just make sure you come through with the promised reward, or motivation will be killed, and trust wounded. It's applying consequences that is tough. When the child breaks a rule, there is a basic sequence to follow when administering the consequence. If you follow these five steps, the corrective process of punishment will be made easier and more effective.

The first step is: Get the facts. This is when you didn't directly witness the event (which is most of the time). Allow your child to tell his or her story. It can be very entertaining. Warn the child up front that if he or she lies, the consequences will be worse. If possible, have your child tell both you and your spouse at the same time. Gather information from others if necessary: other kids, parents, teachers, etc. Take time to get the complete picture. Listen and reflect as the kid talks.

The second step is: Check with your spouse and your support system. When your child has said her piece, put her on hold. If you're married, talk with your partner privately. Agree on the consequences. If the consequence is already written down in the contract, this discussion won't take long. If not, work out your disagreements. When you walk out of your meeting and face your child, a united front is critical. If you're a single parent, call your support system and get some input before announcing your decision. (It can be a good idea, if the consequence is not in writing, to ask your child what she thinks a reasonable consequence would be. She might come up with a better one than you did.) If you're not in a rage, continue, and move to the next step.

Step Three is: Make your opening statement. You'll say something like this: "I am (expressing this emotion) _____ because you (did the following) _____." Share your feelings briefly—very briefly—and calmly. No emotional outbursts. No lectures. No guilt trips. No "After all I've done for you." Save your breath, because the focus is not on you and how bad this is for you. Don't make any personal attacks. Again, if you get angry, you lose! Your anger is a payoff for the kid! Keep the focus on what your child did and the consequences. "This is too bad for you. You made a poor choice, and now you pay the price."

The fourth step is: Apply the consequence. You'll say, "The consequence will be _____." Lay it on her. It's specific, time-limited, and reasonable. You entertain no argument or discussion about the consequence. Be prepared for manipulation. Kids are great actors. My kids ought to have a roomful of Oscars for their touching performances.

Your kid will cry crocodile tears in an attempt to get your sympathy. While crying, she'll be watching you closely for any reaction. You say, "Go ahead and cry. I don't blame you. Here's a tissue." Your kid will blame other people. It's always somebody else's fault. "That teacher never liked me," or, "I was just hanging out with them. I wasn't in on the deal."

The kid will fly into a rage. She'll completely shut down and say nothing. She'll play on your guilt. She might say, "If you hadn't gotten divorced, I wouldn't have problems." She'll threaten you: "I'll never forgive you!" Or, the classic: "I don't love you, and I'll hate you forever!" The best response is: "That's up to you. Life is full of choices. I still love you."

You have arrived at Step Five: Offer to talk. In a low-key way, ask: "Do you want to talk about what happened?" You won't talk about the consequences, but about what the child did. Just make the offer, and don't push. Obviously, this talk happens later, if at all. When you lay the consequences on her, she hates your guts. Take a break, and then go to the child and bring it up again. It's worth a try to see if you can get into why your child disobeyed. What's going on in her head? What's happening in her life? It's a good idea to pray briefly, out loud, with the child. Often, you'll be the only one praying. But, it's an opportunity to express your love and bring God into the picture.

If your kid refuses to tell you the truth about a major situation (sex, drugs, drinking, or breaking the law), bring her life down to a nub until she talks. She will have no privileges of any kind until she tells the truth, the whole truth, and nothing but the truth. You want the whole story: names, dates, and details. Your child's life is at stake, and you need to find out what's going on. Without confession, there is no sense of forgiveness, and change won't occur.

Use a Daily and a Weekly System

It's a good idea to use a combination of daily and weekly rewards and consequences. A daily system keeps the issues in the forefront and can motivate more rapid change. If the child first completes chores, homework, and other behavior you want, you give a reward that same day. Preferably, the reward should come as soon as possible after the completed behavior. If the child chooses not to do what you have specified, you apply a consequence that same day.

To extend and deepen behavior change, a weekly system must also be used. Used the right way, this approach can motivate a child to perform expected behaviors several days in a row. If the child puts together a good week, you reward him that weekend with a bigger prize. If the child chooses not to put together a good week, you lay on a consequence for the weekend. The consequence will be something bigger and nastier than the daily consequence.

Discipline is a very complicated, difficult, and frustrating area. On many days you'll feel just like God did about the Israelites:

> *"All day long I have held out my hands*
> *to an obstinate people,*
> *who walk in ways not good. . ."*
> ISAIAH 65:2

It's easy to give up and think your kids will never learn how to obey. But don't give up. Hang in there. Keep on doing the right things and in time you will be rewarded for your perseverance. You will receive the wonderful blessing promised in Proverbs 29:17:

> *Discipline your son, and he will give you peace;*
> *he will bring delight to your soul.*

In a world that has no discipline and is falling apart, with God's help we can teach our children limits. If we have no one else but God to help us, He is enough.

The behavior-based system I have described is the most effective system of discipline I've ever discovered. It has helped Sandy and me. It has helped many parents I've worked with in therapy and taught in my seminars. God has used it to make a difference in the lives of many parents and their kids. If you use it, it will help you.

NINETEEN

The Truth about Teenagers, and What You Can Do about It

Definition of a Teenager

After years of clinical experience, careful research, and observation, I have developed the definitive description of the typical teenager: The teenager is an intensely moody, irritable creature who has all the symptoms of PMS, a midlife crisis, and manic-depression. . .at the same time.

The teenager eats a diet that would kill any other creature after just several weeks. Hamburgers, french fries, pizza, and candy are the staples. Vegetables are feared and avoided. Studies with rats have proven the toxic nature of the teenager's diet. The rats are fed the basic teen diet, and within ten to fourteen days, they're all dead. They drop like flies. In fact, the researchers report that these rats seem to want to die. They were lifting one dead rat (he was still holding a piece of pepperoni pizza in his little rat fist) out of his cage, when they noticed some strange marks on the bottom of his cage. The rat had written these words in the sawdust: "Please kill me."

The typical teenager lives in filth and disorder. The teen's room looks like the site of a terrorist bombing. *National Geographic* could do a series of documentaries on the various forms of insect life in the adolescent's room. These documentaries haven't been done because scientists cannot guarantee the safety of reporters and camerapersons.

Teenagers usually travel in packs called peer groups. A peer group is a group of young people trying desperately to be unique individuals, while dressing, talking, and acting exactly alike.

But the defining characteristic of the teenager is the attitude. The mean, rotten, nasty, and selfish attitude. They hate the world. They hate you. They hate sunshiny days, flower petals, birds singing, and everything nice. They don't see the glass as half empty. They see the glass as empty, with a bad stain on it, and crushed into a thousand fragments. They are "cool." You, the parent, are a nerd. They are smart. You are an idiot. They know it all. You know nothing.

My point is, the teenager is a very complicated and confusing individual. Dr. Earl Wilson, one of my professors in graduate school, defines a teenager this way: "an adult trying to happen." The main purpose of adolescence is to grow from a dependent, irresponsible child into an independent, responsible adult. This is one of the most difficult transitions in all of life.

Some teenagers seem to just sail through this time period with a minimum of stress and suffering. Notice, I said *some*. As in, not many. As in, few. As in, rare. I wouldn't count on having this kind of teenager. If you're lucky enough to have one like this, you ain't gonna have two! The vast majority of teenagers find these years painful and turbulent. And, of course, so do their parents.

The Big Five

Your teenager has to become an independent, responsible adult and create an identity—all while undergoing tremendous changes in five areas:

- Physical
- Emotional
- Intellectual
- Spiritual
- Social

I call these the Big Five. And believe me, they are big. Have you ever seen one of those old horror movies where the main character is transformed from a normal person into a hideous, grotesque monster? Well, that's nothing compared to what happens to a teenager. Unlike a horror movie on television, you can't just turn it off when it gets too sickening. You've got to live with this transforming creature for at least six years!

That's the bad news. Go ahead and scream in pain. You'll feel better. The good news is, at least it's not seven years. Just kidding. The good news is, you can survive these years and do a great job helping your teenager grow up to be a healthy, maturing adult. What you need to know as a parent is what these changes are and how, specifically, to deal with them.

Hormones on the Loose

The physical changes in a teenager's body are rapid and spectacular. Hormones are literally running wild and produce tremendous changes in general physical development. The growth spurt occurs, making them taller and heavier. The girls usually shoot up first, which makes it tough for the boys. But most of the guys won't be midgets for long. They'll catch up and pass most of the girls a few years later. The boys' voices change and facial and pubic hair sprouts. Acne can be a problem to them—

just when they are so conscious of their appearance!

Hormones trigger changes in sexual development. Girls begin their periods. Boys' and girls' genitals develop and mature. Your teenagers will be completely sexually mature well before the end of high school. But not necessarily completely sexually responsible. Your teens will be able to have sex and produce babies. That's a scary thought, isn't it?

There is a tremendous focus on physical appearance in the teen years. On every survey taken with groups of teens, physical appearance is their number one concern. Nothing else is even close. In fact, physical looks occupy the first ten spots on the list!

It is a fact of life that a teenager's self-esteem is dramatically affected by physical appearance. A teen's constant companion is the mirror. A teenager simply cannot walk past a mirror without looking. Studies have been done to prove it. Teens have been offered fabulous prizes—hundreds of dollars, a new car, a day off from school—if they can just walk past a mirror and not look. They can't do it!

Help Them Feel Understood

What can you do in response to these phenomenal physical changes? I have some ideas that will help you and your teenager. First, help them feel understood. Don't try to convince them that looks aren't important. It's a waste of time, and they'll feel terribly misunderstood. Allow your teenagers to spend an hour and a half getting ready to go out. As long as they aren't late or hogging the bathroom, let them take their time. It's important to them that every hair be in place.

Praise their looks regularly. Say things like: "You look

good." "I like that shirt." "That's a pretty outfit." They won't acknowledge your praise. You won't hear, "Thanks, Mom. I needed that. As you know, physical appearance is very. . ." Dream on. Just keep giving the compliments, because deep down it makes a difference.

Do not—I repeat—do not criticize their looks. Making fun of a certain physical feature is cruel: "You've got Uncle Harry's nose, all right." Do not make negative comments about their hair, dress, or physical features. These kinds of comments are like a dagger in the heart. You are attacking them and crippling them.

Give them the freedom to look and dress as they choose, as long as it's not too outrageous. I draw the line at spiked hair, a ring through the nose, and other bizarre expressions of individuality. Earrings are okay—with me—for both boys and girls, as long as they are in the ears. If my son William wants an earring, I won't be happy. But if his grades and behavior and spiritual life are okay, I'll allow it.

Help Them Look Their Best

Listen to me, fellow parents: Buy them the clothes that are in style. Every teenage peer group has an approved dress code. If your kids don't have the peer-approved uniform, they're spotted a mile away. They don't get into the group! You don't have to like it. It's not right. It's not fair. But it's the way it is. In my day as a teen, my peer group of guys wore brown desert boots. I still wear them. I guess I never really grew up.

I saw a kid in therapy a few years back who was a bona fide nerd. This teenage guy came walking into my office wearing a plaid button-up shirt, white socks pulled up to his knees, and dress shoes with tassels. His parents (who were nerds, too) told me he was having social problems. I thought to myself, *No! Really? I can't imagine why.* I told that kid, "Son, you're a nerd." I didn't tell his parents they were nerds, since they were the ones paying me. The first thing I did was to get him to change his clothes.

If acne is a problem for your kids, take action. You can't stop acne, but you can fight it and reduce its severity. Complexion is critical to your teenagers. Get them to a dermatologist, pronto. It's money well spent. My folks took me when I was a teenager, and I appreciated it. I didn't thank them, but I appreciated it.

Talk about Sex

Don't wait until you give "the talk" about the birds and the bees. That will be too little and too late. If you put it off, your kids will be taught sex by our culture and their friends. I don't think you want that.

Begin early—four or five years of age—and gradually teach them more and more about sex. And please, use the correct anatomical terms. Don't say wee-wee or peeny! It's a penis. Don't say hole or opening. Say vagina. Say clitoris. Do you want your son to say in the locker room, "Yeah, that's my wee-wee!" He'll be humiliated.

Teach God's view of sex at every opportunity. God's view is abstinence. Please join Sandy and me in teaching abstinence. Abstinence means no sexual activity before marriage. This is, in fact, not God's recommendation; it is God's command (1 Corinthians 6:18–20; 1 Thessalonians 4:3–4).

Do not advise your kids to use condoms or any form of

birth control. I can't believe the number of Christian parents making this mistake. This is approving premarital sex and handing your teenagers a license to have sex. There is no safe sex outside of marriage—period! Can you imagine Jesus Christ saying, "Well, I guess you're going to have sex anyway. Go ahead and sin, but just be careful." Never. I believe it is possible for teenagers to choose to refrain from engaging in sexual activity. If they have been involved, it's possible for them to stop. Note: This applies to petting, to sexual activity, in general.

TWENTY

Come Ride My Emotional Roller Coaster

D riven by our old friend hormones and the pressures of the age, a teenager's emotional life is often confusing and chaotic. Crudely put, teens are all over the map. They're bouncing off the walls!

What would be cause for therapy or hospitalization for adults is perfectly normal for teens. Have you heard those radio and television ads describing the problems of teenagers? A deep-voiced announcer reads a list of adolescent symptoms, each of which requires immediate hospitalization. If the hospital chain that produces these ads is right, then every teenager in the world ought to be in a rubber room! Actually, that wouldn't be a bad idea. It's just not feasible. There aren't enough hospital beds.

"My, Aren't We Moody?"

Teenagers experience dramatic, rapid, mood shifts. They can go from happy and carefree to depressed, withdrawn, and angry in fifteen minutes. Their moods are largely driven by circumstances. For example, your daughter talks to her boyfriend Bobby on the phone. She hangs up and is happy as a lark: "Bobby called and we talked. Everything's great!" Then her friend Susie calls with some negative information about Bobby. Somebody saw him talking to a new girl after school!

Your daughter is furious and hurt. But then Bobby calls right back and clears the whole thing up. That girl was just asking directions to the library! Your daughter is happy again. She's back on top of the world! What a roller coaster!

Teenagers are unbelievably irritable. They are highly sensitive creatures who take offense at the slightest remark. Teasing is not appreciated, and you parents need to cut it out during these years. They have no trouble brutalizing you verbally, but you make one comment about them and they fall apart. Their emotions control their behavior. Decisions are based on emotions, not logical thinking.

Just Try Talking to a Teen

It's very difficult—just about impossible—to have a decent conversation with a teenager. Everything you say is twisted and thrown back in your face:

- "Nice day, isn't it?" "You would say that!"
- "You're on the computer?" "Duh!"
- "How was school today?" "How do you think it was?"

No matter what you say, they respond with a sarcastic, belittling comeback:

- "Whatever!"
- "Yeah, right!"
- "I don't think so."
- "You're wrong!"

• "And your point was?"

And, of course, the all-time classic: "You just don't understand!" Wouldn't you love to respond: "No, honey, I don't understand. No one has ever suffered as much as you! Unless it's me, living with you." What can you do in response to these massive emotional changes? I recommend that you move and not leave a forwarding address. (Of course not.) Here are a few practical suggestions.

Patience Is a Virtue

There are a few main mistakes parents make when a teenager is emotionally upset (which is most of the time). First, we get sucked into the emotional intensity of the teenager. This is difficult to avoid because teens are masters at dragging us into their volcano of nasty, violent emotions.

As the teen's emotions escalate, so do yours. Pretty soon, things are out of control, and you've got a messy, emotional battle on your hands. You can't out-escalate teenagers! They can always go up another notch. Emotional escalation is what they're good at. It's what they do!

You've got to stay outside the volcano. If there's any hope of a conversation—some kind of connection—someone has to be the adult and maintain some composure. That would be you. You must learn how to stand in front of the volcano and listen. Don't try to shut down the volcano. You'll get fried! Don't run away from it. That's tempting, but it won't solve anything.

Listen to your teen, because in this way you can avoid getting all hot and bothered. You can keep your blood pressure within normal limits. Also, with one listener, there's a chance the volcano will calm down, and you could have a semi-normal conversation. Maybe.

The second mistake parents make is trying to logically explain the situation. When a teen is emotionally upset, she's nowhere near the logical level and you can't immediately bring her to that level. Men are particularly prone to use logic. Look, men, it doesn't work with our wives. What makes you think it'll work with your teenagers?

Here are some common, logical responses parents use (I've used every one of these):

- "You shouldn't feel that way."
- "Things aren't that bad."
- "You're overreacting."
- "Life ain't fair, kid."
- "Look on the bright side. Without a boyfriend/ girlfriend, you'll have more time to study."

These are well-meaning attempts to reduce the intensity of your teenager's emotion and make her feel better. But they fail miserably! In fact, these logical responses make things worse. Far from feeling understood, the teen feels rejected, because her feelings have been dismissed.

Another logical response is to offer a solution. You say, "Amy, if I were you, here's what I would do." And you give her a nifty solution. Amy responds, "Wow, Dad. I hadn't thought of that! I guess my emotion was clouding my mind. You're so wise and insightful. I feel much better! Come here for a hug." Are you kidding? No way. Amy would be angry and insulted at your solution.

When teens are emotionally upset, they don't want logic. They don't want solutions. They want to be heard. Actually, they don't want to be heard. They want out of the conversation. But they need to be heard.

Reflect, Reflect, Reflect

The only communication tool that works in conversations with teenagers is reflection (as I discussed in chapter 11). Feed back what they say, and feed back what you observe their feelings to be—which shouldn't be very difficult. No matter how outrageous or illogical or distorted they are—and they'll be all these things—let them be. They can't help it! It's a disease! They're teenagers!

As long as they aren't knowingly lying, disrespectful, or screaming. . .reflect. "Steve, you're furious and you say you're going to kill your math teacher." "Susie, you're fed up with life, and you plan to drop out of school, live in a commune, and work at a coffeehouse." "Sharon, you hate your hair, you hate your life, you hate the dog, and you hate me. You're depressed because you think you're ugly and you think you have no friends."

Don't judge what your kid says. Don't analyze it. Don't laugh at it. In fact, don't say anything original. It's too soon in the conversation—or monologue as the case may be—for that. Just reflect, giving back key words, phrases, and emotions. Your teen will try to incite you to react and suck you into the vortex. Don't bite! If you get too intense, you lose. The conversation's over. And you haven't helped; the teen does not feel understood.

Reflection gets you into the conversation. It guides you

past all the pitfalls and hazards of the first few sentences. Talking with a teen is like shooting the worst rapids you've ever seen. Only with a guide can you get through without hitting the rocks. Reflection is your guide. It is your best friend in a time of turmoil.

Reflection helps your teen feel understood. And that's pretty close to a miracle. Understanding is what he needs. He's convinced you can't understand him. You're too old and too out of it. No, of course you're not that old, and you're not out of it.

After you reflect, you'll get your turn to talk. And this is the only way to earn that chance. Just establish the connection and communicate the understanding first. Then, you can say what you want to say. In many cases, the teen will calm down emotionally and actually be able to hear what you say. When she's emotionally agitated she can't listen.

Now, there will be plenty of times your teenager will blow up, rattle off a string of words, and stomp off. This is the machine gun and run approach. You're just verbally riddled. You have no chance to reflect. Or, even if you do reflect, he's in no mood to talk.

How do you get an upset teen to talk when she doesn't want to talk? Wait a while. Don't follow a teen in emotional overdrive down the hall. What, are you crazy? Wait thirty or forty-five minutes, maybe even longer, and then go to her and say, "When you want to and are ready to talk about it, let me know. I'll listen." Then, immediately walk away. Don't try to force her to talk, and don't beg. If she knows you really want her to talk, she'll never do it. That would be violating the teenager's code.

If you get no response, try bringing it up one more time at

the end of the day. Do this one-on-one in the teen's bedroom. Typically, at this time of day most of the mean is gone. You ask her—once—"Do you want to talk?" If she still refuses to talk, drop it. If there are some things you simply have to say about the situation, sit down, say them briefly, and get out.

Parents, Express Your Emotions

One of the ways to build a communication bridge is expressing your emotions in a calm, sincere way, directly to your teenager. Very few parents do this. Share how you feel about your job, the kind of day you had, your hopes and disappointments, and your experiences in your relationship with God. Do this one-on-one. Don't share your deepest secrets—these are for your spouse and another best friend. But tell your teen what's going on in your life and how you feel about it.

This personal sharing is good modeling for your teenager. You're teaching him or her how to express emotions. You're saying, "Here's how you do it. Watch me." Hardly any lesson will help your teen more to achieve emotional strength in his life. Plus, if you expect your teen to share, you'd better share.

Your sharing is good for your relationship with your teen. It helps create a bond between you. When you share yourself, your teen gets to know you—as a person, not just as a parent or an authority figure. It's an expression of love! It's a positive interaction. It's positive communication. For many parents, the only interactions they have with their teenagers are negative. ("Turn down the stereo. Put those things away. Let me tell you. . .")

Share your emotions and a part of your personal life, regardless of their response. You keep initiating. You keep talking. Be brief. Don't rattle on and on. Again, try doing this at night when they're weak, tired, and more mellow. Or do it when they're in a good mood. That will happen about once a month.

Your teenager's not going to say, "Thanks for sharing. I feel like I know you better, and there's a bond between us." But that's what happened! Your teen will act bored to death. That's also part of the teen code. He'll be yawning and staring at the wall. But you go right on sharing, because it's good for both of you. You're building the bridge, and building the bridge takes time.

TWENTY-ONE

Help! My Brain Is Growing

Don't Be Gaslighted by Your Teenager

D irector George Cukor created a masterpiece with his 1944 film, *Gaslight.* Ingrid Bergman (who won her first best actress Oscar for this role) and Charles Boyer play a newly married couple. The beautiful, young but neurotic (and not so terribly bright) Paula thinks she'll live happily ever after with her smooth, charming Gregory. Boy, is she wrong. Soon after the wedding, Gregory begins an insidious campaign to drive Paula insane. In fact, the only reason he marries her is because of where she lives. He knows her dead aunt's fabulous jewels are hidden somewhere in that house.

His plan is to drive Paula nuts and have her committed to an asylum. Then he can search for the jewels at his leisure. And sleazy, sneaky Gregory almost pulls off his cruel, ingenious plan. Step by step, he makes Paula question her sanity. He moves objects around the house, then denies they've ever been moved. Every evening, he dims the gaslights and tells Paula there's nothing wrong with the lights. He takes things from the house and accuses Paula of stealing them. Even the way he says her name, slowly drawing out the syllables—"Paaauuullllaaa"— would drive anyone over the edge.

In a classic scene near the end of the movie, Gregory and Paula are sitting with a group of rich socialites (Paula's friends) listening to a concert. Gregory leans over and whispers,

"Paaaauuuullllaaaa, where's my watch?" You shout at the television screen (this is a rented video): "Tell him to buzz off, Paula! Can't you see what he's doing?" But Paula starts to sweat and tells Gregory she doesn't know. With a smirk on his face, he opens her purse and "finds" his watch. Paula breaks down completely and has to be taken home. At this point, you hate Gregory's guts and can't believe how naïve and dumb Paula is. You're sure Gregory has won.

But just in the nick of time, a kind policeman (played by Joseph Cotton) saves Paula from a terrible fate. The policeman knows what's going on and why Gregory is trying to drive his wife away from the house. He convinces Paula that she's not crazy, and together they expose Gregory, and he—Gregory—is the one sent away—to prison.

The last scene is priceless. Paula, who now knows her mind is sound, finally gets her revenge on Gregory. She teases him unmercifully and makes him think she'll help him get the jewels. She cuts him to ribbons with her biting and sarcastic comments. Great stuff! It always gives you a good feeling when a real dirtball gets what he deserves. Plus, it looks like there's some real chemistry between Paula and the policeman. Some women never learn.

This movie describes pretty accurately what can happen between parents and their teenagers during the adolescent years. The incredible changes in the brains of your teenagers can make you feel like poor Paula—confused, believing that you are slowly losing your grip on reality. Your teenagers, like Gregory, will try to make you believe you are the one whose brain is out of whack. The truth is, they are the ones struggling to make all sorts of intellectual adjustments. What you need to keep your sanity is a kind psychologist who can tell you what's really going on. That's where I come in. I will now describe what goes on in the brains of teenagers and how you can help them through this period of intellectual upheaval.

Three Intellectual Shifts

There are three basic intellectual shifts that occur during the transition from teenager to adult. The first shift is from concrete thinking to abstract thinking. Concrete thinking is the thinking of a child. It is simple, literal, and present tense. Once, I told one of my girls to stop teasing her sister. I said to the girl being teased, "Your sister was just trying to get your goat." The five year old responded, in total sincerity, "I don't have a goat." That is the answer of a concrete thinker.

Abstract thinking is the thinking of an adult. Barring some developmental disability, all adults reach the abstract level. It is complex, figurative, and logical thinking. The abstract thinker can consider the past, the present, and the future.

A concrete statement by a parent would be: "Please do your English homework now." Simple, plain, literal, present tense. An abstract statement by a parent would be: "What will happen to you in the future if you fail English?" The future? What's the future? A concrete-thinking teen has no idea. He can't yet project his mind into the future.

The second major shift is from present-tense thinking to long-range thinking. Most teens think about ten minutes ahead. They are very impulsive. They act on the spur of the moment. They'll throw together social plans at the last minute. "Mary and Bobby just called, and we want to see a movie tonight. I have to leave in five minutes. Can I go?" Or you sit around for hours waiting for some kid to call your kid to confirm possible plans for that day. Most teens lack planning and organizing skills. They have trouble working toward tomorrow's goals, let alone next year's goals.

The third shift is from idealistic, self-centered thinking to realistic, other-centered thinking. Teens are idealistic dreamers. Real romantics. They think about how the world ought to be, not how it is. They fantasize about careers and the life they want to lead. Your idealistic son says, "I'll live way up in the Colorado Rocky Mountains in a cabin." You ask, "Where will you get the money to buy the land and build the cabin? How will you make a living way up there?" He has no idea. He hasn't thought about it.

Teens are also maddeningly self-centered. There is an almost complete focus on self in the teenage years. Your teenager considers himself the center of the known universe. If they discover another universe, he'll be center of that one, too. This is annoying. But it is completely normal. His appearance, his needs, and his life are what occupy most of his waking and sleeping hours. And he expects these personal concerns to occupy your mind. You exist to serve him and his grandiose plans. It takes years for a teenager to see the world realistically and learn how to meet the needs of others.

Now, some practical actions you can take to prepare for these intellectual changes.

Forget Subtlety, Just Ask

Make specific, concrete requests when you want something done. Don't be subtle. Don't hint. Don't take for granted or presume. Give precise instructions. Assume your teen is still a concrete thinker. It's a pretty safe assumption. For example:

"Susie, I want you to complete all your homework and clean the living room before you may use the phone. Come to me when these jobs are done, and I'll check your work. Then you may use the phone for a half an hour. You must be off the phone by 9:30 P.M. Please repeat what I have said."

Allow "Friendly" Arguments

Arguments, or debates, don't do much for you. Frankly, they're a pain in the rear. But they do help teenagers in a number of ways. They give teens the chance to test your beliefs and values as they build their own. This is critical for internalizing values. Of course, you are modeling values. But you also must allow your teenagers to challenge you. They're going to attack your most cherished beliefs in such areas as:

- spiritual truths
- lifestyle issues
- politics
- abortion
- premarital sex
- music/entertainment

You name it, they're going to challenge it. Don't be too threatened. Allow them their opinions, no matter how far off they are from the truth. What do you do when they're attacking values you base your life on? You tell them to shut up! You tell them they're wrong! No, you don't. What do you do? You reflect. (Remember reflect?) Then you state your case calmly.

Back when I was in high school, I challenged my dad on

abortion. I had always been taught that abortion was wrong, that it was killing an unborn child (which is exactly what it is). But I had heard some other liberal views, and suddenly I wasn't so sure. My dad heard me out. He didn't try to change my mind in any direct way. He showed me what the Bible teaches about abortion, the unborn child, and the sanctity of that life, and he urged me to think and pray about it. Dad could handle being challenged, so I felt free to talk to him.

If you can't handle being challenged, your teenagers won't approach you. They won't talk through issues with you. They may end up rejecting your beliefs. They will talk to others outside the home about the critical issues in their lives. These other persons and culture will have more influence than you in these issues. Is that what you want? How many girls have gotten pregnant because they dared not talk to their parents about sex, about male/female interaction, about the ramifications of sexual activity, about the true meaning of love, about why you believe what you believe?

As your kids argue, they also work on their reasoning and logical thinking skills. They need to practice these skills. They need to learn how to think through issues. Don't try to prove them wrong or embarrass them. Even if they are wrong, let them talk. This is tough, I know. It's hard to bite your tongue and cry inside when they're talking gibberish and making no sense and trampling beliefs sacred to you. What if you pop off, and the conversation blows up and ends too soon? Wait a while, then go to the teen and try again. "I'm sorry for losing my cool. What were you saying, honey?" I know it's like taking a beating, but do it anyway.

In addition, arguing with you gives them some valuable relationship skills they'll need in life. How to assertively state their feelings and beliefs. How to disagree with others and maintain the relationship. If they don't learn these skills in discussion with you, where will they learn them? The answer is, they won't learn them. Don't tolerate disrespect or verbal abuse or any unacceptable language, but let them challenge you.

Here's How the Real World Works

You need to teach your teenagers how to live responsibly and morally. You do this by showing them how things work out there in the real world. Don't lecture, but use brief comments on everyday, current events. This helps them learn reality.

My dad was a master of this teaching method. In fact, that's where I got the idea (along with a lot of my parenting ideas). Dad used news stories, television shows, and events in the lives of friends to make points about how life works. He used the lives of real persons—Hollywood stars, athletes, friends, politicians, rock musicians—to show the consequences of sin. What he was doing was personalizing sin. The concept of sin is too broad and it is often lost on kids. So, my dad showed my brother, Mark, and me the face of sin:

"I see where these two stars lived together for a while and now are breaking up. They're in a nasty custody battle over their out-of-wedlock child. Living together is sure a mistake."

"I heard that Brandy, a senior at your school, is pregnant now. Her boyfriend dumped her, and she may have to drop out of school. Premarital sex sure changed her life."

"Look at this in the paper. That famous rock star overdosed on alcohol and drugs yesterday. I guess if you play with that stuff, you get burned."

Dad wouldn't even ask for a response. He'd just comment

and drop it. The message he sent, and that I received, was: "You disobey God, you get suffering and pain. . .every single time."

You can also personalize victory. Point to those Christian celebrities, athletes, and friends who follow God's laws and receive blessing and honor. I greatly admire A. C. Green, the basketball star, for his public stand against premarital sex. I've told my kids about him. Dave Dravecky, the baseball pitcher who lost his pitching arm to cancer, is a wonderful example of Christian courage and faith.

If you have the intestinal fortitude, use your own life as an example. When you disobey the Bible, tell your kids the consequences: "I didn't go to that friend who hurt me. Now, we're distant. I'm calling him this week. I'm sure that's what God wants me to do." When you are walking with God and obeying Him in a specific situation, let your teenagers know! "I refused to do business with that man because he wanted me to break the law. God has honored me by blessing me with a lot more business from honest persons."

TWENTY-TWO

Show Me How to Walk with God

There's No Gold in Them Thar Hills

I n 1876, a young man decided to join the Gold Rush. He had the fever, and he had it in a big way. He just knew he was going to strike gold in the mountains of the American West. He convinced his new bride to join him in this great adventure. They staked their claim on the side of a mountain in a remote, desolate area. He sank a shaft and began working his way into that mountain.

Day after day, week after week, and month after month, he toiled in his mine. The initial excitement wore off, and he realized it wasn't going to be as easy as he had thought to get rich. He did find gold, but only enough to meet the basic needs of his family. His wife gave birth to two children, and they built a pretty good life out there by the mountain.

Near the end of his third year of mining, he began to find a strange substance in his shaft. He'd never seen it before. It was almost pure white and soft. He could mold it and shape it with his hands. As he dug, he found the white material all through his mine. It was everywhere! The more he dug, the more he found. He cursed his bad luck! He wanted gold, and gold was black in the rock, not white! He threw the useless white stuff to the side as he continued to dig for gold.

Year after backbreaking year, the miner dug out the guts of

his mountain. Year after year, he found huge quantities of the white substance and only small amounts of his precious gold. He always made a living and provided for his family, but he never hit the big gold strike he'd always dreamed about.

Finally, after forty years of digging, he called it quits. His kids were long since grown and moved away. It was him and his wife now, and they weren't getting any younger. He hated to do it, but he put his mine up for sale. Amazingly, the very first man who came to inspect the mine wanted to buy it. He seemed downright eager to make the deal.

The old miner shook the buyer's hand, signed the bill of sale, and began to walk away from his mountain, for the last time. He stopped, turned around, and said to the new owner: "You'll have to spend quite a bit of time cleaning out that white stuff. There are great piles of it all through that mine." The new owner laughed out loud and shouted, "You fool! That white stuff is silver! You just sold me a mine worth millions! You had the biggest silver strike in this state under your nose for forty years, and you didn't even know it!"

So many parents, like this miner, don't realize that they have something of enormous value right under their noses. They know it's there, but they don't know its worth and what to do with it. Parents, this priceless resource is your spirituality. A personal relationship with God is the greatest, most significant part of your life and your teenager's life. Don't ignore it! Don't give it lip service. Use it. Develop it. The primary source of effectiveness in helping your teenager survive these years and become a healthy adult is spiritual growth.

Get Ready for Rejection

There's nothing more crucial than building your teenager's faith. If there is a God—and there is—then there's nothing more essential than establishing a relationship with Him and growing in that relationship, through His Son, Jesus Christ. Your teenagers must move from your faith to their faith. Guess how they're going to do that? They're going to question your faith. They're going to challenge your faith. They're going to pull away from your faith. They're going to compare the world's values to your values.

It's a ragged, messy process. It's supposed to be. Your teens are going to reject your faith as they build their own. They'll test your faith to see if it is real to you. Here are some practical strategies to guide your teenagers to a strong faith of their own.

Be a Living, Breathing Christian

At the center of modeling is sharing your personal walk with God with your children. You need to open up and let your teenagers look inside. You need to demonstrate how your faith works every day. You want to give your teens a God-consciousness. Everything done in life—everything—is about God and for God. You want them to learn that they exist to love, serve, and glorify God.

Passive, arm's-length modeling won't accomplish these spiritual goals. The best way to build your teen's faith is with active, involved modeling. Too often, parents teach the Bible, but they don't show their kids how it applies to their own lives. If you don't regularly connect the Bible to your life, your kids will think it's just a dry, dusty old book written for people who lived thousands of years ago. To teach them that the Bible is

God's living Word for today, show your teens how it works in your life.

Children do not learn values and spiritual truth by being taught. They learn them by emulating their teachers.

Start sharing, in short bursts, your personal, daily walk with God: your spiritual victories, your spiritual defeats, how you apply what you are reading in the Bible to your life, and how you are becoming intimate with God. You don't reveal the most personal details of your life but enough to show your kids how a living, breathing, honest-to-goodness Christian operates. What you're doing is discipling your kids.

Show your teenagers exactly how you do your quiet time. I can remember my dad telling me how he did his morning devotions. Just making sure I saw him doing his devotions wasn't good enough. He had to teach me how to do it. He described how he began in prayer: adoration, confession of sins, thanksgiving, and ending with supplication (a fancy name for making requests of God). He showed me the prayer list he used, the devotional books he liked, and how many verses he'd read at one time. If my dad hadn't taught me how to do a quiet time, it would have taken me years to figure it out. He made it easy for me.

Pray spontaneously with your kids. Don't just pray at mealtimes or during family devotions. How do you develop an intimate relationship with someone if you talk with that person only at certain brief, limited times? Paul teaches us to "pray continually" (1 Thessalonians 5:17). So, to live out this command you need to pray more often. Pray as issues and concerns come up. Pray for yourself, your kids, and others. Pray with your kids at home, in the car, at night before bedtime, in the kitchen before school, and on the phone. The message is:

"When you have a concern, take it to God right away." (See Philippians 4:6–7.)

Share your Christian faith with others, and let your kids know you're doing it. In some cases, you can even do it together. The Bible urges us to share our faith with others. "Witnessing" is simply telling others what Jesus has done for us. In His last words to His disciples, Jesus said, "Go and make disciples of all nations. . . ." (Matthew 28:19). Pray with your kids about those you are talking to about Jesus and tell them how the process goes. This kind of modeling will also serve to teach your teens how to share their faith.

Family Devotions Made Easy

I've already mentioned (in chapter 13) the principal elements of successful family devotions: once a week, twenty to thirty minutes, read the Bible, make it personal, make it practical, and include prayer. I want to add some specific how-to's that will make your devotional meetings lively and effective. (Even though I'm focusing on teens in this chapter, these ideas can be used with kids of all ages.)

Always have one of your kids read the Bible passage or the devotional selection. Then briefly teach the biblical principle and apply it to your life. This kind of personal sharing is the prelude to asking your kids to apply the principle. Let's say the verse you're applying is Ephesians 4:26: "In your anger do not sin." You can say something like this:

"I was very angry with Bobby earlier today. I yelled at you, son, and that's not what God wants. I'm sorry, Bobby. You still get the consequence, but I was wrong to yell."

Or, if you are applying Ephesians 4:15, "Speaking the

truth in love. . ." you can say:

"I had a conflict with Mrs. Roberts at church. I prayed about it and went to her this past week and talked about it. With God's help, I spoke the truth in love, and I feel much better now."

Now, you can't always tell a personal story based on a portion of Scripture:

> "Thank you for reading the story of Cain killing Abel, Melissa. Kids, this may shock you, but I killed a man twenty-five years ago. I spent some time in the big house, and I. . ."

Usually though, you'll be able to personally apply the Scripture passage. If it applies to your life, it will also apply to your kids' lives.

To draw your kids into the Bible passage and motivate them to respond to it, try using small groups. Divide the family into groups of two or three and give each group an application project based on the passage. Then, after five minutes or so, each group reports their findings to the family. Your question for the groups could be as simple as: "What would you do if this situation happened in your life?" or "Tell the family a time when you did what this verse tells us to do."

For teens, it's effective to describe specific, real-life scenarios for them to respond to in their small groups:

- You're at a party, and someone offers you a beer. What do you do?
- A friend of yours says to you, "There isn't any God." How do you respond?

- Your girlfriend asks you to cross the line sexually. What do you do? What Bible verse would you use for support?
- A classmate asks you to let her look at your test answers. How do you handle that? What would Jesus want you to do?

To stimulate participation in the application and prayer times, it's a good idea to "seed the crowd." Before the devotional meeting, ask one of your kids to speak up when you ask for input. When one family member participates, it usually breaks the ice and others will feel free to join the discussion. Also, during prayer ask each person to pray for the family member to his right. This connects the family, makes the experience more personal, and builds relationships.

Occasionally, you can share portions of videos. There are many excellent Christian materials these days, and videos typically command and hold attention. Your Christian bookstore or church library will probably carry a variety of videos. Focus on the Family has a number of superb resources in the video area.

If you have a creative flair, dress up like a biblical character for the devotional time. (This is especially fun for younger kids.) Get an old bathrobe and a pair of sandals, and you're ready to go. You could be Moses, Paul, Peter, or Mary Magdalene. Please, none of you dads dress up like Mary. We don't want to confuse the kids. For about twenty minutes, you become the biblical person. You can read a Bible passage "you" wrote, and take questions from the audience. It isn't every day your kids get a chance to ask Moses a couple of questions. ("Why did you smash those tablets? Most people break one commandment at a time. You broke all Ten Commandments in one fell swoop.")

Play Twenty Questions

Let your teenagers know they can ask you any spiritual question, whenever they want to. They need to ask questions, because it's one of the main ways they challenge your faith. As Dr. Howard Hendricks told one hundred of us seminary students in his Bible Study Methods Class, "There are no stupid questions." Your teens will ask the same questions new Christians and spiritual seekers have been asking for centuries:

- Is Jesus Christ the only way to God and heaven?
- What about the millions of devout persons in other faiths like Islam and Judaism? Don't they have the truth, too?
- How can we really know Jesus died and rose from the dead?
- Is the Bible really inerrant? I've heard some people say it has mistakes.
- What about all the people, like isolated tribes of the world, who never hear about Jesus? Where do they go when they die?
- How could a loving God allow the terrible suffering in the world?
- How about all the hypocrites? If these persons (pastors, televangelists, Christian musicians, and athletes) really knew Jesus, how could they commit such terrible sins?

And on and on, the questions will come. Let them come. Expect them to come.

Encourage your teenagers to ask questions. Give the best answers possible. If you don't know the answer, say so. Tell your teen you will do some research and get back to him. Ask your teen to do a little research on some of his questions. Give him some helpful books and a few pertinent Bible passages. Your church library, and often the public library, will have reference books. Church staffs are always happy to answer questions and recommend materials. Work together with your teen as she struggles to answer these critical questions about God and the Christian faith.

Keep Your Teen in Church

It frustrates me when Christian parents allow their teenagers to stop going to church. They tell me, "Well, they're old enough now to make this decision. We don't want to force them to go, because it will turn them off." Wimps! That's what these parents are! There are times to stand up and be a parent, and this is one of them. Yes, you do need to force your teens to continue to attend church. Church attendance is a nonnegotiable item. As long as they live in your home, they'll go to church and to youth meetings.

They need to learn about God. They need to worship God. They need to build relationships with other Christian kids. They need healthy, fun, and safe activities in a Christian environment. They need to know that God is important to you, and because of this, there will be no compromise in this area. When your teens crab about going to church, tell them what my dad told me: "If there is a better place to be on Sundays than church, we'll go there."

Parents, be involved in the youth group. Do what you can to help with organization, transportation, chaperoning, and crowd control. Know the leaders and what they're teaching your teens. Talk with your teens about youth group and what they're learning. Sometimes, it is necessary to allow your teenagers to attend a youth group at another church. If a youth group is poorly run, dead as a doornail, or has just a handful of kids, you may have to find another group for your teens. These years are too critical to let your kid languish in a subpar youth ministry. If you cannot bring about change in your church's youth group in a reasonable amount of time, bail out.

TWENTY-THREE

Peers Are
My Priority

Shoved to the Back Forty

O h, the joy of being the parent of young children. You are
the very center of their world. They deeply love you. You
are their hero, and they are in awe of you. You are larger
than life. Your life is interesting. For them, everything you do
is terribly exciting. You know everything. They want to be just
like you. Their one goal in life is to be with you. They are desperate for your love. You are the wind beneath their wings.

Oh, the cold reality of being the parent of teenagers. You
are rudely shoved to the back forty acres of their world. They
barely tolerate you. You are not too impressive a person, and
they are embarrassed by you. You are smaller than a pygmy.
Your life is boring. For them, everything you do is about as
exciting as watching hair grow. You know nothing. They want
to be the opposite of you. Their one goal in life is to get away
from you. They are desperate—not for your love—but for your
money. You are the bad smell in their nostrils.

All of a sudden, your teenagers can't be seen with you in
public. Their worst nightmare is being spotted by a friend
while you are in their company. It's the kiss of social death.
When you ask them to go out with you, to eat or shop, they
cringe, and say in a pleading voice: "But somebody might see
me with you!" You look in the mirror to make sure you haven't

turned into some kind of hideous monster. No, you look the same. You can't even pick your teens up at school anymore. They ask you to park around the corner, out of sight. They race to the car, jump in, hunch down low, and yell, "Drive!"

Their whole lives revolve around their peer group. Their peers are cool, adventurous, exciting, and so much fun to be with. They constantly think about what their peers think of them. All they want to do is talk to their friends and spend time with their friends. You aren't even considered in their social plans. You have been totally eliminated as a social option. They own your phone. When it rings, you are mowed down in their mad scramble to get to it. Of course, it's silly of you even to think a call might be for you. The phone is never for you anymore. What friends you still have can't reach you by phone. The line is always clogged with your children's vast network of teenage cronies.

Peers on Center Stage

This not-so-subtle rejection of you is part of a massive social shift that takes place during adolescence. Your teenagers want to get as far away from you as possible and as close to their friends as they can get. You have been replaced by the peer group. Your kids move away from you and attach firmly to their friends. For the first time, peers take over the central place in the teenager's life. Parents are still important, but you now share the stage with peers.

This shift is perfectly natural and normal. It needs to happen. It is, however, a painful shift for both parents and teens. For parents, it's a loss. Your children are growing up and leaving you. It's also scary. Just when all these changes are happening to your kids, they break away from you! For teens, the fear of rejection by peers is incredibly intense. The teenagers' world is a jungle: the popularity game, the cliques, the pecking order, and the many insecurities. It's hard making and keeping friends.

The move toward the peer group is painful for both parents and teenagers, but it is absolutely critical. It is the only way for teenagers to begin the process of genuinely breaking away from parents. It is the only way for teenagers to establish their own identity and independence. Here are some things you can do to help your teenagers make this major transition of their lives.

Make Your Home a Refuge

During the teenage years, your home needs to be a place of love and acceptance. A safe retreat from the world and its pressures. A sanctuary. Even if your teens aren't around much, they need to draw strength and security from the environment at home. In war, there is the front, and there is the secure home camp behind the enemy lines. When your teenagers drag in from the fighting, their wounds need to be treated. They need rest and peace. That's your job as parents. Then, after "R & R" (rest and relaxation), they're ready to go back into the battle.

If you are married, work on your marriage. During your children's teen years, it's essential to maintain a strong, intimate relationship with your partner. If your marriage is struggling, get help, and get it now. Moms, if at all possible, be at home when your teenagers return from school. Your presence is just as important—if not more so—now than it was when they were children. My mom was always home when I came home from school as a teenager, whether it was early in the afternoon or after sports practice. She was my rock, my security, and my encourager. Since I was a teenager, I didn't tell her how important her presence was to me. But I appreciated her being there. I needed her to be there.

Help Your Teen Build Relationships

Do what you can to help your teenager connect with his peers. His independence and emotional health depend on developing healthy peer relationships. Do not allow your teen to withdraw and become a loner. That is not only unacceptable; it's dangerous. If your kid doesn't learn how to make friends now, it's likely he never will. Do you know how the baby eagle is taught how to fly? One day, the adult eagle sneaks up behind the baby and kicks it out of the nest. Somewhere between the nest high on a rocky crag and the ground, that baby eagle learns how to use its wings.

The social area is another area in which you need to take assertive action. Push your teenager to be involved in Sunday school, the church youth group, school sports, and other activities populated by peers. There are excellent parachurch organizations like Young Life, Student Venture, Youth with a Mission, Youth for Christ, and Fellowship of Christian Athletes. Solitary pursuits are okay, as long as your teenager has plenty of time with peers. If your teen is really struggling socially, you can try doing things with other families who have teens.

Respect Their Choice of Friends

Some of the kids your teenagers hang out with will turn your stomach. You'll be convinced their friends are not good enough.

They're not quality choices. You want your teenagers to be friends with the best the teen world has to offer. Good, decent, moral kids who comb their hair (which is short), smile a lot, and sit in the front row in church. I mean, why can't they be friends with the pastor's kids, the president of the youth group, the valedictorian of the high school, and the kid who went on a mission trip to a leper colony? Come on, get real. Remember, you don't choose your teenagers' friends. Your teenagers choose their friends.

What you can do is to get to know their friends. Have your teenagers invite their friends over. Don't hang out with them and make yourself a pest, but find out what they're like. If you comment on a friend, you'd better be low-key and careful because if you protest and criticize too strongly, you will achieve just the opposite; you will push your child toward a less-than-acceptable companion. If you have solid proof of a friend's acting out in a major area such as drinking, using drugs, occult activity, breaking the law, bad language—take action immediately. Tell your teen to cut that friend off, pronto. That friend will now have to earn his way back into the relationship by proving real change over time.

There are times when teenagers get connected with the wrong crowd. If you find your teen running with a bunch of lowlifes, you can't afford to do nothing and just hope for the best. Something has to be done. Scripture very powerfully warns against bad associations in unmistakable terms: "Do not be misled: 'Bad company corrupts good character'" (1 Corinthians 15:33). If your teen stays with this kind of peer group, she will go down the tubes.

If it's a school-based peer group, remove your teen from the school and put her in another one. It's a dramatic move, but could very well save you a lifetime of grief and very possibly your teen from ruining or even losing her life. If these undesirables are in the neighborhood or church, you can apply stiff consequences for any contact with them. You then work with your child to help her develop a new peer group.

Let Your Teenagers Go

Don't hang on to your teens, because if you do, they will not establish their independence. Also, you'll cause tremendous rebellion as they attempt to get away from you. Find ways to allow them to exercise freedom and responsibility. You have to expose your children to the culture and to the world system. They're going to have to live in it by themselves someday soon. Know where they are, who they're with, and when they're coming home, at all times. Supervision is as vital now as it was when your children were very young. In a very few short years (though it will look like an eternity), this primary job will be over. But at the same time, let them move away from you with confidence and a growing independence. Encourage them in this process.

So, You Want to Date?

Dating is a privilege. It's a reward. It is not a right. It must be earned with impressive effort:

- Good grades
- Household chores being done
- Good behavior at home and school
- Responsibility demonstrated

- Respect for parents
- Spiritual and moral life good

You add dating only to a life that is spiritual, balanced, and healthy. Not a perfect life, but a very good life. If there are any slips, any poor choices, you yank dating immediately.

You don't allow single dating until sixteen years of age. I've never seen a case where under sixteen was a good idea. Teens—despite what they think—simply aren't ready emotionally. They haven't even formed their own identity yet. You'll push your kids into sex if you allow them to date too soon. Even with good sex education—which is crucial and also your responsibility—we are dealing with raging hormones, with a natural drive that is akin to nuclear power. Am I getting through? Every study I've read reports that a very high percentage of junior high kids who date will have sex before their high school graduation. The same studies found that this percentage is lowered significantly for kids whose parents made them wait until sixteen to date. Of course, we don't need to have studies to give us this information. It's common sense!

You allow your teenagers to date only Christians. And not Christians in name only. Oh, no! You'll make sure these kids definitely know Jesus Christ and are walking with Him. You'll ask these questions of potential dates:

- "Are you a Christian?"
- "What makes you a Christian?"
- "Do you attend church weekly?"
- "Are you growing spiritually?
  What steps are you taking to grow spiritually?"

You don't demand perfect Christians, but you want solid Christians. It's so easy for your kids to fall in love with non-Christians. They can get used to adjusting to a non-Christian. It makes it more likely they'll eventually marry a non-Christian. Plus, dating a non-Christian weakens their spiritual commitment. And don't even begin to accept your teen saying that he will win this person to the Lord. This is another area in which the stakes are extremely high. You must be diligent.

You interview all applicants, boys as well as girls. If you're married, you both sit down together to conduct the inquisition—I mean, questioning. This interview should not be held just before a date. You're not going to ask a few questions while the car is running. No way. This is not merely perfunctory. This interview isn't even held the same day as the tentative date. This is a pre-date interview. When it's over, there may not even be a date.

You'll ask questions, and you'll get answers. You'll ask not just the spiritual questions listed above but questions in other areas. You want the would-be dater to meet the same requirements you've set for your kid: grades, chores, behavior, moral life, etc. You make sure your kids know these requirements, so they won't even try to drag some shaky customer in front of you.

Just like a job interview, you thank the applicant for coming. Tell him you'll let him know. You tell your kid, "If any kid who wants to date you has a problem with the interview, then that kid isn't worth your time."

Do not allow your teen to get obsessed with a boy or girl. Make sure your kid has, before beginning to date, a balanced life: friends, activities, a happy, healthy connection to the home and you. You limit phone calls and time together. Dating is only a part of their lives, not all of it. School, God, church activities, family, and forming their own identity are all more important than dating.

My Time Line for Dating

Dating, in my opinion, begins in the middle school years (sixth, seventh, and eighth grades) with group activities involving both sexes. You can allow—even encourage—your twelve-, thirteen-, and fourteen-year-old kids to engage in youth group at church, youth group activities, school clubs, parties, and having friends over to the house. These gatherings should be supervised by a responsible Christian adult every time. At this age, you do not allow unsupervised time with the opposite sex. They cannot "hang out" at the mall with a coed group. In this stage, they're just getting to know the opposite sex in a general way. If they are attracted to someone, see that it stays very low-key. Phone time with the opposite sex is okay, but again, it should also be low-key, and not excessive. Phone calls should be limited to ten or fifteen minutes in length.

The next stage is group dating. This can happen in ninth and tenth grades—roughly fifteen and sixteen years of age. This provides more time for your teens with the opposite sex. They can be with one member of the opposite sex, but in group situations such as: youth group church meetings, youth group activities, school parties, and parties in your home or at a friend's home. Again, adult supervision is maintained at all times. You know the kids in the group, and you know the supervising adults.

In group dating, there is no touching. There is no going out alone together. There is no deep commitment in the relationship. You do not allow double dating until your teens are sixteen years old. If they double-date, they'll start out as a foursome and then split up into couples. We're not idiots, are we? We must not be idiots. At all times we have to be one step ahead of them.

Let's say your Susie likes Timmy and vice versa. They can talk on the phone. They can E-mail within reason; don't look over their shoulders, but supervise. They can even say, "We're going together," or "We're going out." But they see each other only in a group setting. Timmy can come to your house, but it'll be the whole family together. You do not allow Timmy and Susie to spend time alone. Even at this level, you hold the interview with Timmy.

Single dating comes next in the progression. This is for teenagers in grades eleven and twelve (sixteen, seventeen, and eighteen years old). Just because your kid hits sixteen, he or she doesn't automatically begin single dating. In addition to the other requirements I've mentioned, your kid has to have successfully moved through the first two stages of dating. If your kid hasn't had exposure to the opposite sex in group settings, then your kid isn't ready to date one-on-one.

Also, be very wary of a big age difference. I particularly don't like older boys dating younger girls. One year might be okay, but not two or more. Oh, I wonder what a nineteen-year-old man wants with a sixteen-year-old girl! Not conversation, I can tell you that. The older boy—even if he is two years older—better be the next Billy Graham.

The last stage I call serious single dating. This is dating beyond high school. Your child is at least eighteen or nineteen years old, in college or working. This is usually the time when real intimacy can develop and a mate is chosen. Here, you still have opportunity for some input. But your child is an adult and should make her own decisions. I am not a believer in so-called "courtship dating." (By "courtship dating" I mean an arrangement in which the parents have a huge say in who their adult children date and marry.) Look, once your kids are adults, they can date whomever they want to date. If you've done your job well, they'll be fine.

There are few things in life as difficult as living with a teenager. Unless it's living with more than one teenager. These principles I've shared will enable you to survive the experience. Better yet, these action steps will improve your relationship with your teenagers and help you make a real difference in their lives.

TWENTY-FOUR

Living in a Blender: Strategies for Blended Families

You Got Siblings, You Got Rivalry

L et me make one thing perfectly clear right up front. Sibling rivalry is normal. It's a fact of life. Get used to it. All kids fight. I laugh when I read child-rearing "experts" who believe sibling rivalry can be largely eliminated. What kind of a fairyland are they living in? These authorities are either incredibly naïve, have never lived with children, or have watched too many episodes of *Little House on the Prairie*. The very first siblings, Cain and Abel, had a pretty bad case of sibling rivalry. Hopefully, your kids won't go to the extreme of murder, but you can count on plenty of rivalry.

I can speak from personal experience. My brother Mark and I had a great home environment. We had terrific, godly parents who loved us and practically wrote the book on good parenting. But Mark was my brother, so I hated him. We fought like cats and dogs for years, especially during the junior high years. There was a continual stream of verbal jousting. Everything we did became a gigantic life-or-death competition.

Just getting into the car was a huge contest. I had to get there first, and I had to be in the front seat. (And to think I have the nerve to get upset with my kids over their car wars.) We had countless physical fights, too. I never won a fight, because Mark is two years older and was always bigger and stronger. Being zero and five hundred in the ring against him made me hate him all the more.

But the main source of my bitterness toward Mark was his popularity. Mark was the undisputed king of the youth group at Christ Community Church. I was the Invisible Man—okay, *boy*. Mark had girls literally hanging on him all the time. I failed to see the attraction. It was like he had some strange power over adolescent girls. He had a string of girlfriends. There was a line of girls waiting for their chance. I'm telling you, it was like a harem! He had tons and tons of dates. I had nothing, none, nada, zilch. Girls weren't exactly beating a path to my door. It was awfully cold living in Mark's babe-magnet shadow.

To my credit, I took all this in stride. I was actually happy for Mark. I mean, he was a great guy and deserved female attention. He was a good Christian, so maybe this was God's way of rewarding him. I prayed that he'd get as many dates as possible. Here, I know that you know I'm kidding. My resentment burned inside. I hated him for his popularity. I prayed—out of my junior high mentality—that he'd develop horrible bad breath and no girl would go near him.

I was able to get some revenge. I was always better at school and sports. You'd better believe I played up these two bright spots big-time. At report card time, I was in my glory. When I did well on the athletic field, I was riding high. I acted as though these academic and athletic achievements completely satisfied me and balanced things out with Don Juan. I never let on that I was jealous. But frankly, I would rather have had the chicks.

Take what I've just described between my brother and me, multiply it by 10,000, and you're close to the level of intensity in a blended family. The jealousy, the rage, the guilt games, the leftover pain from the past, the insecurities, the confused feelings, and the divided loyalties, are all mixed together in one simmering pot. You've got all the ingredients for a nuclear chain reaction.

There aren't words adequate to describe the massive adjustment a blended family must undergo. It's not even close to *The Brady Bunch* television show, where all the petty squabbles were worked out in thirty minutes. It's a lot closer to World War III, with missiles and bombs and trench warfare and casualties.

Even though it's a very tough road to go down, you blended family parents can achieve success. God wants your new family to become a cohesive, integrated unit. He will be faithful to help you. I've counseled a lot of blended families, and I know you can reach the peace and stability you want. In the following pages, I'm going to share some of the blended family strategies I've seen work in my clinical practice.

Expect the Worst

So many of the remarried couples I've seen have made the mistake of thinking everything would work out just fine in their new family. Before the marriage they tell me, "Dave, our kids get along great! They seem excited about the wedding. And we're each clicking with our partner's kids." I say two words: "Just wait." They think I'm crazy. They're sure their blended family will be the exception. Two months after the wedding, they are back in my office crying, "Help!"

Do not entertain for a moment the fantasy that your transition will be a breeze. It won't be. It will be a painful, brutally hard adjustment for everyone involved. Even your pets will need therapy. Expect nothing less than vicious, industrial-strength sibling rivalry. It's all part of the adjustment. The rivalry between your biological and stepchildren will be nastier and last longer than the rivalry between biological siblings.

By getting married and throwing all your kids together, you shatter their carefully constructed family order. Kids base much of their security in a pecking order, a clearly defined chain of command, as well as the rituals and patterned rhythms of family life. All this is gone when the two of you get married and you all move in together. Now, the kids have to start all over establishing a new system.

A further complication is the fact that, in most blended families, you have different combinations of kids living together at different times. You have this kid only on the weekends, another kid one week on and one week off, and another kid all the time. The process of creating a stable family structure takes a lot longer due to the different schedules. Reentry, when a kid comes back to your home from another home, is a particularly chaotic and stressful time.

So expect the worst. Give the process plenty of time. On average, it takes a good two years to fully adjust, and this includes the extremely difficult aspect of grieving the incredible loss of the original family. I'm not kidding. Be prepared to step in and stop sibling rivalry that gets out of hand. Don't allow physical fights to continue when it's obvious one child will get hurt. Don't allow cruel verbal abuse to pass without applying a serious consequence. When you do not witness a conflict between two kids, punish both.

Deal with Past Pain

Please understand that your new family has been formed only

because of losses. These losses have to be addressed and worked through. Make sure everyone has healed or is healing from the trauma of a divorce, or loss of a parent through death, that caused the broken family. Many parents try to move on too quickly, and they then pay a dear price in their new family. Never play down or disregard the great loss the children have sustained and are still suffering.

If the parents are not recovered and are still emotionally tied to the ex-partner, that baggage will transfer to the current marriage. If the children still have emotional pain from the loss of the previous family, that pain will transfer to the natural parent and the stepparent. Especially to the stepparent.

Many remarried couples focus on all the new crises and problems in the blended family, instead of addressing the still very present unresolved grief that's at the root of the turmoil. For example, I see in therapy a blended family in which eleven-year-old Amanda is at the center of a hurricane of conflict. Amanda hates her stepfather and is doing everything in her power to make his life miserable. I find out the reason for Amanda's behavior is she hasn't grieved the loss of her natural father. She sees him only every other weekend, and it's killing her inside. She feels it is a betrayal of her natural dad to get along with— even accept—her stepdad. She still harbors the magical wish that someday her biological parents will get back together.

You parents must openly model your recovery from the loss of a previous spouse and the separation from children. Not being able to live every day with your own children hurts, and that hurt needs to be expressed. Express your emotions in front of your natural and stepchildren. Express your emotions individually and in family meetings. Family meetings are even more important in blended families. Allow yourself to be spontaneous with your grief, anger, and hurt. When such emotions come up, let them out. Of course, encourage the children, both one-on-one and in family meetings, to grieve their losses and express painful emotions.

Your Marriage Is Number One

To have success in a blended family, you need a strong, healthy marriage. Your marriage is the foundation on which, over time, the kids will build their security. To survive the first two years and get to the good stuff, you must make your marriage the most important relationship in the family. Putting your marriage in the Number One slot is exactly what God wants you to do (Genesis 2:24; Ephesians 5:25). You will face an astronomical number of adjustments, compromises, and crisis interventions. If your blended family marriage isn't a great marriage, it has no chance at all. Because of natural feelings of guilt over a divorce, many new partners focus on the kids to make sure they're happy, and end up neglecting their new marriage. That's a bad idea. Many children, consciously or unconsciously, want to sabotage your new relationship. For example, your biological child tries to end this marriage by forcing you to choose between her and your new marriage partner; quick, what do you do? You choose your marriage partner. If you choose your child, you have dealt your blended family a mortal blow.

Do all the things necessary—anything—to keep your marriage relationship intimate and fulfilling and fun. (I remind you again about my book, *Men Are Clams, Women Are Crowbars*, published by Barbour Publishing, and I suggest you read it together.) Work on your communication skills, because you're going to need them. Make time each day to be alone for talking and touching. Keep the romance alive. At least once a week, go out on a date.

Talk privately about everything that comes up with the kids. When I say everything, I mean everything. Particularly in the first year of adjustments, the kids need to see an absolutely united front. You must be the best team you can possibly be. You are Fred Astaire and Ginger Rogers. You are George Burns and Gracie Allen. You are Laurel and Hardy. Actually, you'll feel like Laurel and Hardy sometimes, but don't show it in front of the kids. In front of those kids, who are watching your every move, you are Siamese twins joined at the brain.

When a situation that requires discipline comes up, put the kid or kids on hold and talk about it in the bedroom or in the car in the driveway or on the phone. Hash out your disagreements and come to a joint decision. Explain to the children what you are doing. This is good modeling for them to see, too. If you can't agree, then do nothing until you can agree. As many times as humanly possible, present your decision to the kids together. The kids need to see—in person—real unity. As you deliver your decision, stand together or sit close together. The biological parent of the kid in question is the one who announces the verdict.

Biological Parents Discipline Their Biological Kids

A classic mistake many new stepparents make is jumping right in and disciplining their partner's kids. This inflames resentments already smoldering inside your stepkids. They'll scream, "You're not my mom!" or "You're not my dad!" They're right; you're not. And you have no business applying your own consequences to stepchildren. For at least the first two years, biological parents discipline their biological children. Every time.

Now, obviously, there are plenty of times when the stepparent (usually the mom) is the only parent on the scene. The biological parent can't be reached, and something has to be done. If it's a major situation, and the biological parent will be home later that day, then put the kid on hold and wait. When the biological parent shows up, have a parent conference as soon as possible. After the meeting, you sit together in front of the child. But the biological parent applies the consequence.

If the situation is fairly minor, or the biological parent is out of town for a while, the stepparent must handle it. Still, you try to reach the biological parent by phone to discuss the problem. Whether or not you speak with the natural parent, when you apply the consequence, you do it only as the representative of the natural parent. In other words, you make it clear that the punishment is coming from the biological parent, and not from you. "I've talked to your dad, and this is what he told me to do." Or "I believe your dad would want it handled this way."

Later, when you do discuss what happened with your partner, he is free to change the discipline if he feels it is necessary. I recommend giving the biological parent the prerogative of deciding how to discipline his or her own child for at least two years. You know your kid better than the stepparent does.

But there are two other good reasons for this approach. One, a child will accept discipline much more readily from his own parent. Knowing his biological parent will continue to be his disciplinarian gives a child a sense of continuity and stability. It keeps the line of command clear to him, and there's less (note, only "less") chance he'll react with hostility toward the stepparent. Two, keeping the stepparent out of directly administering discipline gives the new step-relationship a chance to grow. A stepparent who disciplines too quickly will not develop a good relationship with a stepchild. I have seen no exceptions to this rule.

That's What Friends Are For

One of the main reasons you don't discipline your stepkids directly is so you can build a friendship. There is nothing more important in the first two years—except your marriage—than working on the relationship with your nonbiological kids. You need to do everything you can to bond with them. You have no biological or historical bond, so you're going to have to work steadily and patiently to form one.

Patiently is the key word. Your stepkids will make it very hard for you. Part of them wants and needs a connection with you. But a much bigger part of them wants to deny you any hint of friendship. Be prepared for massive and persistent rejection, because that's what you're going to get. Don't ever give up. In the face of almost constant failure, keep trying. Spend time with them. Have fun with them. Invite them to do fun things they enjoy. Ask them about their day, their friends, and their interests. Pray with them if they'll permit it. Accept their rejection with as much grace as possible and keep coming back for more. It may take years to achieve a breakthrough, but it's worth the effort. This is unconditional love at its most difficult.

Understand that you are not the child's mother or father and never will be. You are an adult who will serve in the parental role in this family. There is a big difference, and all kids know the difference. Do not force or even encourage your stepchild to call you "Mom" or "Dad." Don't do it. Your first name is appropriate. If a child eventually chooses to call you "Mom" or "Dad," fine.

Don't try to stepparent without a support system. Every stepparent must have at least one support person of the same sex who is also a stepparent. You've got to scream, complain, and whine about your stepkids, and you can't very well do that with your spouse. The venting, the prayer, and the advice will save you and get you through.

Team-Building Is Critical

Your job is to mold a complex, diverse group of kids into a team. To accomplish this goal, you've got to engage in a high number of team-building exercises. The more you do, the better. It's like throwing spaghetti against the wall: Some noodles are bound to stick.

Family meetings are team-building exercises, and you need to hold a lot of them. In the first year, I recommend at least two family meetings per week. It's critical to stay on top of the rapid changes in the family system. The rule in every family meeting is: Anyone can say anything as long as it's expressed in the appropriate way. For example, fourteen-year-old Brittany may feel free to share her anger, even hatred, with her stepmother, as long as she does not attack or show a lack of respect.

Of course, you make prayer a part of every family meeting. You need to model the truth that both of you are not depending on yourselves but on God. You want your kids to understand that they don't help the family improve for you or for themselves. They do it for God, to please and obey Him.

Parents need to model by venting their own honest feelings

about how things are going in the family. If the parents and kids don't express powerful emotions in family meetings, they'll express them in destructive ways outside the meetings. These family meetings also deal with compromises, adjustments, discipline, and ideas from all members as to how to improve things and resolve impasses. The family meeting isn't the only team-building exercise. Here's a list of other creative ideas to build unity in the family:

- Take a lot of fun trips outside the home (amusement parks, public parks, the beach, the zoo, the video arcade).
- Be a team and play other families in sports and games (baseball, football, soccer, bowling, scavenger hunts, car rallies).
- Divide the family into different teams and set up competitions between or among the teams (board games, charades, potato sack races, card games, hide-and-seek).
- Spend time with successful stepfamilies so they can model what is working in their families.
- Give big-time praise and rewards when you catch your kids getting along (not for being nice, but just for getting along and not trying to kill each other).
- Give out prizes once a week to the children who have contributed to family harmony (a trip to a favorite restaurant, an extra snack, one day without chores, five bucks).

Dealing with the Ex Factor

I'm sure all of you reading this chapter have a wonderful relationship with your ex-husband or wife. It's a mature, understanding relationship, built on trust. You've put aside your differences and can work well together for the sake of the kids. Yeah, right! A good relationship with an ex is a pretty rare commodity. What's much more common—almost the rule—is a running feud filled with bickering, competition, confrontations, and petty games. It can be worse than sibling rivalry. You can't control what your ex does, but you can control what you do.

Don't bad-mouth your ex, no matter how tempting or how much he or she deserves it. Be honest and express your feelings about him or her with your kids, but don't make any personal attacks. This could put you on your ex-spouse's level and keep the revenge game going. It motivates your children to defend the other parent. Plus, this kind of reaction teaches your kids that bad-mouthing is okay. Don't allow your ex to continue to ruin your happiness.

Do the best you can to develop a working relationship with your ex. This will, of course, depend on how he chooses to behave. Do not tolerate disrespect or verbal assaults. After saying you do not think attacks, insults, etc., are right, if you are on the phone, tell him you will hang up unless it stops, and if talking in person, walk away. Show as little emotion as possible. Don't let him know he's getting to you. Just like a child, he's trying to get a reaction out of you. So, don't give him a reaction. Try to remain cool and controlled and reasonable.

Don't let your child manipulate you by using your ex as a weapon. Avoid spending wars. Some ex-partners will try to buy the kids' love and loyalty. In your home, other than birthday gifts and other special situations, your child has to earn rewards. Learn how to respond when your child threatens, "I'll go live with my dad." If the child is young and a move isn't even feasible, ignore the threat and try to get at the feelings behind it. With an older child, you still make an attempt to help her express what's going on inside. But to take that card of manipulation out of her hands, you might say, "Well, that's a big decision. If you think and pray about it for a week, and are still serious, we'll start to talk about it. We'll look at all the factors and see what the best decision is." Sometimes, letting a kid go to your ex is a good idea. Sometimes, it's not. If a child does go, it's only after long discussions and times of prayer. And she has to go for a significant period of time—six months, minimum. You don't create a revolving door.

To avoid a breakdown in discipline, you and your new partner try to establish the same behavior standards (as discussed in chapter 15), in both homes—yours and your ex-spouse's—for your children. You make an attempt with your ex to agree on uniform standards, but it will likely fail. You explain to the children that you expect them to meet your reasonable standards no matter whose home they're in. If your kids disobey a rule at the other parent's home, even if your ex allows the behavior, you will apply consequences when the child returns to your home. Of course, you'll have to hope your kids tell you or you find out in some other way. This isn't a perfect system, but life isn't perfect. It at least maintains the integrity and continuity of your system of discipline.

TWENTY-FIVE

The Greatest Man I Ever Knew: A Message to Dads

"When Daddy Ain't Happy. . ."

One day, among my appointments, I talked with three married women at my therapy office. Each woman talked about her husband, the father of her children. Each woman cried as she told me her story. At the end of the day, a thought struck me: These women had painted a picture of a main weakness in many fathers.

The first woman told me this: "Dave, my husband is hardly ever home. During the week, he leaves very early each morning and gets home late at night. He's a workaholic and is completely absorbed in his career. He brings work home and often works on the weekends. There are many days he doesn't even see the kids. He could be a great father, but the kids and I will never know, because he's not around."

The second woman said, "My husband does a good job of getting home from work. He watches his schedule and is home with us a good deal of the time. The trouble is, he's present, he's in the building, but he's not really at home. He's preoccupied and caught up in his own interests. He watches television, reads the newspaper, works on the computer, and does projects in the garage. He doesn't play with the kids. He doesn't talk to them. The kids and I joke that we have a cardboard cutout dad, but it's not too funny."

The third woman said, "Dave, my husband is very good at playing with the children. He throws the ball, plays board games, and horses around. I appreciate this. I really do. My problem is, I have to do everything else for the kids. I make their meals. I clean up after them. I wash their clothes. I get them ready for school and church. I help with their homework. I discipline them. I talk to them about personal and spiritual things. I lead family devotions. I'm tired of carrying the whole load alone. I am completely exhausted. I want some help!"

I ask you: What weakness do all three stories illustrate? It is the unconnected father. The father who has no personal relationship with his children. I'm convinced most fathers struggle in this area. I know I do.

You've heard this little saying, I'm sure: "When Momma ain't happy, ain't nobody happy." So true. There's another little saying which is just as true: "When Daddy ain't happy, ain't nobody cares." The reason nobody cares is because Dad is outside the family mainstream. He's a bit player. He's unconnected.

After seeing these three ladies, I was able to speak to each of their husbands. We sat down in my office and talked about fatherhood and how they were doing as dads. These men weren't bad men. They weren't evil men. They weren't maliciously trying to hurt their children. In fact, they loved their children. The problem was, their children didn't feel loved.

You can love your children all you want, Dads. But if you don't communicate that love to them, there is no love. There can't be any love apart from a personal, connected relationship. I told these dads that when a father is not personally connected to his children, three things happen. And they're all bad. I'm going to tell you dads what I told them.

Dads, You Personally Suffer

You lose three valuable things when you are unconnected to your children. First, you lose the opportunity to enjoy your kids. It's great fun to play with your kids! It's stimulating, interesting, and stress-releasing. Some of my best times have been with my kids: playing in the pouring rain, baseball in the front yard, horseback riding in Colorado, hitting golf balls down the street, playing Barbie dolls with my daughters. . .

Second, you lose the opportunity to learn from your kids. We teach our children many things, but they teach us many things as well. That is, if we are connected to them. Emily is a lot like me: high-strung, passionate, and impatient. She has my weaknesses. To help her in these areas, I have to work on myself. Leeann is kind, sensitive, caring, and warm. I need more of these traits. As I interact with Leeann, I improve in these areas. Nancy is independent, a free spirit, spontaneous, speaks the truth, and lets the chips fall where they may. Thanks to Nancy, I'm learning in these areas. William, my son, is motivating me to be a better man. I want him to see, as much as possible, how a godly man lives.

The third thing you lose is your legacy. Your enduring legacy is not your job. It's your children. Fifty years from now, people won't be sitting around your office talking about how much you meant to the company. And even if they did, so what? Who cares? You are replaceable in any job. You are not replaceable as a dad. You can have a lasting impact, a positive legacy that you pass on to your children. You live on in them!

Dads, Your Marriage Suffers

It means the world to a woman to see her kids connected personally to their dad. She knows how vital this is to the well-being of her children. As well as modeling general values and positive masculine characteristics, it also means the world to a woman to have her husband's help in the practical areas of raising children. It's not fair and it's not right to expect your wife to shoulder the load. And, frankly, most of us dads do that, don't we? Except maybe on Mother's Day!

Oh, she'll do it. Somebody has to do it. But she'll be tired and resentful. I don't know about you, men, but I don't really enjoy having a tired and resentful wife at the end of the evening. It's like coming up against the Great Wall of China or a polar ice cap. If you want some warmth, some softness, and some conversation at the end of the day, guess what you need to do? Help her with the kids! Some of you are thinking: "Oh, that's why she's so cold in the evenings." Yeah. That's why.

Dads, if you're not personally involved with your children, life goes on. Your wife won't kill you as you sleep. She probably won't leave you. But she'll hurt inside. She'll lose respect for you. She'll lose love for you. She'll pull away from you. Not all at once, but over time. This isn't her fault. It's your fault. A woman can't respond any other way. I've never heard a woman say, "My husband isn't personally connected to our kids, but I don't care. I love him more every day."

Dads, Your Children Suffer

As fathers, we have tremendous influence on our children. Influence that will last a lifetime and even affect their eternity. My professional work as a psychologist, my research, my study of the Bible, and my personal experience, all show that fathers play a pivotal role in four essential areas of a child's development.

Your child's self-esteem depends on you, Dad. Am I worthy? Am I likeable? Am I smart? Your child will get the answers to these questions from you, Dad. I've seen many men and women who are broken and feel worthless, because they never got Dad's approval. Don't let that happen to your child.

Your child's competence and self-confidence depend on you, Dad. How your child sees the world and work comes largely from interaction with Dad. Studies show that an involved father improves the academic achievement of his children. Whether or not your child becomes a productive member of society will be powerfully influenced by you.

Your daughter's relationships with men depend on you, Dad. If a girl doesn't have a personal, positive, active relationship with her father, she'll have a difficult time developing a good relationship with any man. This is true of boys and establishing friendship relationships with the opposite sex, too. They don't know how because you didn't teach them.

Your child's relationship with God depends on you, Dad. A child cannot distinguish between God and his human father. A child with a distant, poor relationship with Dad will struggle for years to get close to a heavenly Father. Now, that's a powerful statement. But I assure you, it's true.

I see many adult clients who have problems because of a poor relationship with their fathers. With God's guidance, the therapy process works. These persons can heal and recover from a dad who didn't do his job well. But it's costly, emotionally and financially. I'd be happy to work with your children, Dads, when they're young adults. I don't think you want me to do that, though. Dads, you could save them from that pain and expense, and from years of troubled minds. All it takes is you—being there, being a dad.

Plan A is to prevent problems and pain in your children by being a good dad. And that means building a personal relationship with your children.

Good News for Dads

Well, enough bad news. The good news is, if you become personally connected to your kids, you can turn these three negatives into positives. Instead of suffering, there will be growth and health! The whole picture changes. And it's never too late to start. Our gracious God gives us the chance to make up for our mistakes.

Speaking of God, He's the best reason to get personally connected to your children. He wants it to happen. In verse after verse in both the Old and New Testaments (Exodus 12:24, 26–27; 13:8; Deuteronomy 6:5, 7; 1 Timothy 3:4; and Ephesians 6:4, to name just a few), God instructed the Israelites and all believers after them that dads are to be intimately involved in their families. When God issues a command, He always provides the power to get it done.

Five Things to Do to Be a Great Dad

You dads are thinking: *Okay, all right, you win. I'm overwhelmed by your logic and insights. You've convinced me. I need to be personally connected to my children. How do I do it?* I'm not going to tell you all the specific things you need to do to be a great dad. I've already covered the most important steps in chapters 1 through 24. Dads, I'm just going to ask you to do five things. If you'll do these five things, I guarantee you'll be a great, connected dad in no time.

Number One, ask your wife how you're doing as a dad. Ask her to be gentle and not tell you everything at once. She'll know, because women know just about everything that goes on in a home. She knows her (your) kids and can tell you exactly how you're doing in the fatherhood (and stepfatherhood) department. Humble yourself and ask. And not just once. Ask her regularly—once every two or three weeks. It's a great way to keep on track.

Number Two, ask each of your children how you're doing as a dad. They certainly know. Ask each child how you can do better. Ask what they need from you as a dad—on a personal level and not just as a man who goes to work every day and fixes things and provides for them. Ask them at least every two or three weeks.

Number Three, ask your best male friend how he thinks you are doing as a dad. Tell him to be honest and pull no punches. Ask him how you can improve. Ask him to check on your fathering once or twice a month. If he's open to it, you ask him the same questions once a month about his fathering. ("As iron sharpens iron, so one man sharpens another" [Proverbs 27:17].) I have this kind of relationship with my great friend, Rocky Glisson. Every Saturday morning, we meet and ask each other the tough questions. This has made a huge difference in my personal life, my marriage, and my role as a dad.

Number Four, ask God how you're doing as a dad. Since He knows everything, who could be better to ask? Ask Him to reveal the truth to you. He'll do it. God's Spirit, called the "Spirit of truth," and "the Counselor" (John 15:26), will "guide you into all truth" (John 16:13). Ask Him to help you do a better job. He'll do that, too. He is more interested in your role as a father and the happiness and well-being of your wife and children than you are. If you don't have a personal relationship with God, He has made it easy to establish it. Believe that Jesus Christ, God's Son, died on the cross for your sins, and rose from the dead. Ask Jesus to forgive your sins and to come into your life. He'll do it, and you'll never be the same. You will have the power—God's power—to be the best dad your kids could ever have.

"That Christ died for our sins
according to the Scriptures,
that he was buried,
that he was raised on the third day. . . .
Believe in the Lord Jesus, and you will be saved. . . .
Yet to all who received him,
to those who believed in his name,
he gave the right to become children of God."
1 CORINTHIANS 15:3–4; ACTS 16:31; JOHN 1:12

Number Five (even if it is a bit anticlimactic): If you haven't done it already, read the rest of this book. Focus particularly on chapters 10 through 14, the sections covering the needs of children. Make sure your wife sees you reading this book. She'll be impressed. You'll be her hero. We dads need everything possible going for us.

Dads, let's all make Joshua 24:15 our motto:

"But as for me and my household,
we will serve the LORD."

There's no better way to serve the Lord than to be a great dad. The stakes are high, men. Very high. I know you're up to the challenge. When you become connected to your kids, you personally will benefit. Your marriage will benefit. Your children will benefit. But, best of all, God will be pleased and He will honor and bless you.

So. . .let's get to work.

OTHER RESOURCES BY DAVID CLARKE, PH.D.

To schedule a seminar or
order Dr. Clarke's audiotapes and videotapes,
please contact:

DAVID CLARKE SEMINARS

www.davidclarkeseminars.com

1-888-516-8844

or

Marriage and Family Enrichment Center

6505 North Himes Avenue

Tampa, Florida 33614